Dr SHEWELL-COOPER'S
BASIC BOOK OF
GREENHOUSE GROWING

BASIC BOOK OF
GREENHOUSE GROWING

W. E. SHEWELL-COOPER

MBE, NDH, FLS, FRSL, Dip.Hort.(Wye), DLitt

BARRIE & JENKINS
COMMUNICA-EUROPA

First published in 1978 by
Barrie and Jenkins Ltd,
24 Highbury Crescent, London N5 1RX

ISBN 0 214 20499 5

Printed litho in Great Britain
by The Anchor Press Ltd, Tiptree, Essex

Phototypeset in Great Britain
by The Anchor Press Ltd, Tiptree, Essex

Contents

TO
MONKTON COMBE SCHOOL

A public school with a definite Evangelical Christian background. My Alma Mater and where my sons were educated also. It was there under the Rev. G. F. Graham-Brown, later Bishop of Jerusalem, that I learned to write.

My two grandsons now attend this excellent school.

List of illustrations

Preface

Those who get bitten with the gardening 'bug' are never satisfied until they have a greenhouse. Here they spend hours – often far longer than they need – for glasshouse culture is very fascinating.

To help them with this useful and often profitable hobby I have written this simple book. I hope I have provided what I have been asked to do by many correspondents and that is a guide to the greenhouse both for beginners and maybe too, for the more experienced.

I am most grateful to Miss M. Walpole, BSc(Hort.), Mrs Roy Johnson, DipHort (Swanley), and Miss Maria Dehn, BSc(Hort.), NDH Technical Assistants to The International Horticultural Advisory Bureau, for all the work they have done to make this book a success. Captain M. Mason, who was at one time my Horticultural officer at the Army Horticultural Training Centre, Maidstone, was most kind in reading the proofs and making suggestions. Miss Grace Brydon, BSc(Hort.) corrected the original proofs carefully and my thanks go out to her also.

My Horticultural assistant, Mr C. F. Fraser-Smith gave much thought to Chapters 2 and 3.

Thus did many experts help in the 'building up' of this Basic Book. I hope it will prove useful.

Mrs B. Lovelock, my present secretary, typed every word of the book carefully and successfully. My thanks are due to her.

W. E. SHEWELL-COOPER
Director

The International Horticultural Advisory Bureau,
Arkley Manor,
Arkley,
Herts.

1 The growing of plants under glass

Most people start gardening without a greenhouse, but inevitably they find themselves buying one or building one. This urge for a glasshouse is quite natural, for it enables the keen gardener to keep 'on the go' the whole year round. The greenhouse is a nice place to work in on a cold day. Plants on benches are a godsend to those who are 'getting on', for it saves them bending or kneeling down.

Under glass the gardener is enabled to grow all kinds of plants indigenous to warmer climates, thus increasing the range of plants that he can grow, with the result that it gives him a greater interest.

The plants in a glasshouse should be grown in the conditions as near as possible to those in which they would be growing normally outside. In the chapters dealing with the plants, care has been taken to give details of watering, temperatures and ventilation so that the beginner will have no difficulty in giving the conditions necessary.

The glasshouse enables a grower to force plants out of season. In Chapter 8 and 9 details are given of how vegetables and fruits may be grown successfully for out of season periods – tomatoes in the spring and autumn, lettuces and French beans in the winter – peaches and nectarines early in the summer – strawberries in the New Year and so on.

The greenhouse is also invaluable for raising plants of a half-hardy character, and as soon as the weather is warmer in May and June, the plants can be put outside. The result is that much earlier flowering is ensured, and so the gardener gets a much more beautiful garden for a longer period. It is also an excellent aid to the production of good salad crops. It would be impossible to grow those 3-lb and 4-lb onions without the greenhouse, for it is here that the seeds are sown in boxes also, while many of the particularly delicious vegetables like New Zealand spinach, sweet corn, and aubergine (egg plant) have to be grown under glass first of all if they are to be used early outside.

Those who want continuity of colour in the house will find

the greenhouse a great boon. It enables chrysanthemums to be grown and flower right up to Christmas; all sorts of bulbs may be forced and grown on for the New Year, while there are a host of flowering plants, as will be seen in Chapter 12, that can be grown to provide plenty of colour all the year round.

Foliage plants, including the ferns and the palms, are also useful for house and conservatory decoration, and these are grown in the greenhouse to perfection. Cacti and succulents are very fascinating and a nice airy greenhouse is just what they require.

Some will want to grow orchids, and it is intended to include a future volume in the Basic Book series on cultivating easy orchids. Many of the orchidacae are not difficult to manage in the amateur greenhouse. They are fascinating in their growth habits, and, apart from providing an extra exotic touch, are ideal for the man who wants a nice buttonhole every week in the year.

Years ago only the rich could afford greenhouses, but today they are no one's monopoly and almost every garden has its own glasshouse, however small. One has only to look at any group of allotments in any country to see the number of small glasshouses that the allotment holders have put up during the last few years. The greenhouse has become a necessity, and it is a good thing that this is so, for it does make all the difference, and is conducive to a happy and contented gardener.

When the beginner starts gardening he is usually quite satisfied to cultivate the land outside, but soon he feels the urge to have a frame in which he can raise plants early, and in which he can save the roots of certain plants during the winter. The frame soon leads to the greenhouse and once he has a greenhouse he realizes what extra wonderful pleasures gardening can give! One small greenhouse often leads to another or a larger one for no garden is complete without a greenhouse structure in which a man can work when conditions outside are not suitable.

Conditions in the greenhouse should be as near as possible to the conditions in which the plants normally grow outside. It is a great mistake to 'coddle' plants. They should be given plenty of air. They should not be overwatered and the moisture content of the atmosphere of the house should not be too high. Each plant wants slightly different conditions and so in a house devoted to more than one class of plant, it is preferable to produce the average conditions under which all can live. There are greenhouses in which there are separate 'compartments' which can be kept at different temperatures and different degrees of humidity, but these are rather expensive and are what the small growers may aspire to later on.

In the following chapters brief details are given of the great numbers of plants which it is possible to grow under glass.

2 Construction

Glasshouse building is today a science and it is recommended that all who are considering building, should go to well-known firms who specialize in this type of work. A builder or an amateur cannot be expected to have the knowledge of those who have studied this special subject, and have over half a century's experience behind them. There are too many intricate points connected with the construction which are only learned after many years of practical experience.

The first point is to decide whether a movable or permanent greenhouse is desired. In the case of the former, glasshouses erected in sections and secured by bolts can be purchased, the erection of which is a simple matter that can be dealt with by an amateur. In the case of the latter, a brick foundation is usually essential for satisfaction and permanency, and if a wall is built to where the glass starts, so much the better.

All such brickwork must be on a scientific foundation. The thickness of the walls must be according to a long and high span, or else the weight of the construction will cause the walls to bulge, or the foundations to move if of insufficient dimensions. For the strength of the foundations there is the subsoil to consider, and many other considerations, which only an expert connected with the glasshouse firms can judge satisfactorily.

LOCAL BUILDING LAWS
A word would not be out of place here to remind the reader that these cannot be ignored.

A glasshouse is an exempted building in most districts, but this does not preclude the purchaser from notifying the local authorities of the intention of its erection, and they have the power to disallow the erection of a wooden base house if adjacent to any dwelling house or neighbouring property.

A brick base house is usually allowed in any position subject to the brickwork being carried out in 9-in. work in suitable foundations, and the structure does not interfere with external ventilation of a living-room if placed against a dwelling house.

14

Here again, a building firm should settle any legal point which may arise. A tenant should make sure he has a written agreement with his landlord. In the case of a movable construction, this is most important, as at the termination of the tenancy, the tenant may find he is no longer the owner of the greenhouse.

TYPES OF GLASSHOUSES

Before attempting to describe the construction of a glasshouse there are many points to take into consideration. For instance, in deciding upon a glasshouse, it is necessary first to consider the plan of the garden, the available space, walls and especially the path of the sun, and also the nature of the crops to be raised.

It is because of these various factors that there are many types to consider, but those for general use can be reduced to three main classes:

(1) The Span-Roof
(2) The Three-quarter Span Roof
(3) The Lean-to Roof

The decorative conservatories are altogether another problem.

(1) *The Span-Roof House* is the most popular and certainly the most useful.

It will readily be seen that this house is an equal span building with the ridge in the centre and each gutter or eaves line being the same height from the ground.

(2) *The Three-quarter Span House* is of unequal dimensions, the ridge being approximately two-thirds towards the back wall, which is usually about 25 per cent higher than the front eaves or gutter line.

(3) *The Lean-to House* has the ridge placed directly against the back wall, the height of which should be equivalent to the continuation of the roof of the span or lean-to carried up until it reaches the point where the rafter would meet the wall. In other words the pitch of roof should be maintained at approximately 30° until the wall is reached. A roof slope less than this will cause water to work up through the laps in the glass sections, and condensation will also drop from the glass onto the plants below instead of running down it.

In actual practice, a lean-to house is seldom the cheapest

A Marley acrylic-coated 'Lincoln' lean-to greenhouse

to build, and many existing walls are far more suitable for the building of a three-quarter span glasshouse. For example, lean-to rafters must be increased in size or strengthened and even special bracing is required if the span is of considerable length.

The novice certainly needs the advice of the expert as to the advisability of constructing any of these three houses and also his advice, from an efficiency and economic point of view, as to which of them would be the more suitable.

THE USES OF THESE THREE TYPES

Analysing the uses of the above types can be done briefly, as follows:

(1) *The Span-Roof* type is the most useful. It is designed to be placed in that part of the garden which receives the early, midday and late sun. Light being of vital importance, the span glasshouse obtains the full amount of light possible, and enables full benefit to be obtained both from the morning and afternoon sun. The equal distribution of such light is of great importance in the cultivation of plants under glass. In this type the plants are not likely to be drawn towards the lightest

side of the house. Besides the best light, the span house also affords the maximum space.

It is quite independent of any other buildings or walls, and is used for general plant cultivation and occasionally the wider spans, say of 16 ft to 20 ft, are used as vineries or peach houses.

Economical and efficient heating, too, is a definite consideration, for all space is usable in this type of glasshouse, and there are no high empty spaces, walls, etc., to consume heat.

(2) *The Three-quarter Span* is confined to a space in the garden with its long roof facing south, and the back wall sheltering the house from the north winds.

It has the advantage of trapping more sun than the lean-to house.

This type is also suited for general plant work and can also be used for vines and peaches with advantage with say only 12 ft in width, as the long front roof is very suitably adapted for this purpose.

(3) *The Lean-to.* The usefulness of this house is not to be compared with the above two types because all plants are apt to be drawn towards the light.

It is most suitable for vines and peaches owing to its longish span of roof, but may also be used for general plant work if care is taken in situating the various plants at their correct distance from the glass, building the inside stagings so that the back staging – that is, the one against the wall – is as near the glass as is consistent with the subjects to be grown.

CONCRETE IN GREENHOUSE CONSTRUCTION

The handyman, who likes to do things himself, will find that concrete is the best material to use for the floors and walls of his greenhouse. One of the main advantages of using concrete is that it is permanent and does not require much upkeep.

CONCRETE FLOORS

For this type of greenhouse that is similar to the portable garage, it is advisable to lay a concrete base which also serves as the floor.

By following a few simple rules anyone can lay a satisfactory concrete floor.

The floor should be at least 4 in. thick and the concrete should be composed of 1 part of Portland cement, $2\frac{1}{2}$ parts of clean sharp sand, and 4 parts of broken stone or shingle graded from 1 in. down to 3/16 in.

LAYING THE FLOOR

The site of the greenhouse should be marked out on the ground and this can be accomplished quite simply with the aid of wooden pegs and string. If the greenhouse has timber sides the top of the floor should be about 2 in. above the surrounding ground level.

The ground should be dug to the required depth and the sub-base properly rammed to form a firm and even bed for the concrete. If the ground is of a clayey nature, then it is advisable to spread 2 or 3 in. of ashes or similar material on the ground before the concrete is placed.

When the site has been prepared the framework, which consists of four lengths of timber, say 4 in. × 2 in. is laid on the sub-base and held in position by driving pegs into the ground around the outside of the frame that is formed.

If it is only intended to lay a concrete path or walk down the centre of the greenhouse, this can be laid after the house has been erected. The concrete should be divided into bays, the length of each not exceeding twice the width of the walk. Each bay should be divided from the next by inserting a thin length of timber or damp-proof coursing.

MIXING CONCRETE

In order to obtain the best results, great care should be taken over the mixing of the concrete.

The materials should all be measured in a suitable receptacle such as a bucket. The $2\frac{1}{2}$ buckets of sand are first measured and then mixed with 1 bucket of cement until there are no grey streaks to be seen.

This mixture of cement and sand is then added to the measured quantity of broken stone or shingle, and the whole mass turned over three or four times. The water is then added, and the mixing continued. Do not use too much water as it will make the mixture too sloppy.

The frame is then filled with the mixed concrete, which should be well consolidated with a stout length of timber or a home-made rammer. The length of timber is drawn along the top of the frame to smooth the surface, which can also be gone over with a wooden float. The surface must on no account be overtrowelled as this brings the fine material to the top and tends to result in a dusty surface. It is advisable that a layer of waterproof paper be placed between the sub-base and the concrete slab. This is to prevent the loss of moisture from the underside of the slab while the concrete is hardening.

If it is proposed to use timber for the walls or superstructure, holes should be formed in the concrete whilst it is still plastic in order that bolts for holding down the house may be grouted in at some later date. Suppliers of greenhouses generally provide instructions, and these should be followed closely.

CURING THE CONCRETE

There are still many people who believe that concrete hardens by drying out. Actually the reverse is true, as it is the presence of water which causes concrete to harden and therefore the floor should be covered with wet sacks or similar material to protect it from drying winds and the sun. The covering should be placed in position as soon as the concrete has hardened sufficiently so that the surface is not marred, and kept damp for at least seven days. Alternatively, the floor may be covered with waterproof paper which will retain the moisture in the concrete.

FOUNDATION WALLS

It will generally be found economical to construct the walls of the greenhouse in concrete. These walls, as a rule, are only 3 or 4 ft above the surface of the ground and may be constructed either of concrete blocks or of concrete laid in situ.

The walls should stand on a concrete foundation or footing which should be set below the frost line. A general rule for foundations is that the width should be twice the thickness of the wall. Thus the pressure due to the weight of the wall and any load the wall has to carry is distributed over a greater area, ensuring the stability of the structure.

The foundation should be about 9 in. thick and the concrete should consist of 1 part of cement, 3 parts sand, 5 parts broken stone or shingle.

When the site of the walls has been marked out, a trench should be dug following the outline of the walls. It should be about 12 in. wide and from 15 to 18 in. deep. The concrete should be deposited in this to a depth of 9 in. and before it hardens the surface should be roughened to form a key between the base and the wall.

If the greenhouse is comparatively small then the foundations for the walls may be combined with the floor by increasing the thickness of the concrete at the outside of the slab.

WALLS

To build the walls *in situ* it will be necessary to erect framework or shuttering, which is most easily made of timber. The important point is to ensure that the shuttering is sufficiently battened and strutted to prevent it from moving or bulging whilst the concrete is being placed.

Before placing the wall concrete, which should consist of 1 part of cement, $2\frac{1}{2}$ parts sand and 4 parts of broken stone or shingle, the surface of the footing should be well washed and wetted, in order to remove any dirt and wood shavings that may have fallen in between the shuttering.

The concrete should be placed in layers about 6 in. thick and each layer should be well tamped to effect consolidation.

THE GLAZED SUPERSTRUCTURE

If the framework for the glazed portion of the greenhouse is to be of wood, bolts to which a wood sill may be fastened should be cast in the top of the wall during concreting.

THE SPAN HOUSE

The span house may be a purely portable type with a wood base usually 2 ft 6 in. high with glass sides above, about the same height, making say 5 ft in all to the gutter or eaves line.

The length and width are, of course, optional. It is, however, possible to have a standard wood base house 12 ft × 8 ft × 8 ft to ridge, 5 ft to eaves and this is a very serviceable size for the small garden.

This house is timber framed throughout and is glazed with 24 oz glass bedded on bottom putty (no top putties being used).

The house may have a brick base construction and with heavier timbers in consequence but the same method of construction is employed.

Fig. 1 shows the three-quarter span type house described under that heading. Its construction is readily seen.

THE ALUMINIUM HOUSE

Good aluminium glasshouses are constructed of hot-dip galvanized, cold-rolled, mild steel loadbearing sections with extruded aluminium glazing bars and gutters, and rigid, exterior grade, PVC capping strips. All parts exposed to the

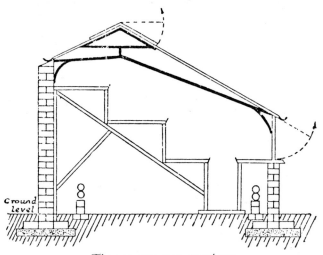

Three-quarter span greenhouse

atmosphere are corrosion-resistant. Base walls are normally concrete blocks or bricks.

GLAZING

This is, without doubt, the most important feature of glass-house design. Most conventional metal glazing bars have the web outside. In this configuration they act as radiator fins, dissipating heat to the outside air. Such a design can very easily present an exposed surface of 82 sq. in. for every foot run of glazing bar.

If there is a wind blowing, the heat loss is considerable.

The Edward Owen glazing system has the web of the glazing bar *inside* the house and the top of the bar capped by an insulating plastic cover strip. Heat loss by conduction through the glazing bars is virtually eliminated.

The large panes of either 3 mm or 4 mm glass are butted together using a specially designed 'H'-section strip. These strips in the roof are arranged to coincide with the narrow-section steel purlins so as to minimize areas of cast shadow. Butting the glass has two advantages. It eliminates those areas of overlap which become opaque with age and of harbouring micro-organisms. Secondly, it is a further source of heat conservation.

VENTILATION

Manually operated ventilators give the maximum open areas.

3 Heating

The utility and success of a glasshouse, however well it may be constructed, depends on an efficient and dependable heating installation.

It is impossible to lay down any hard and fast laws on the subject of the size of the apparatus needed. The advice of an expert should be sought before embarking on any outlay as regards this matter.

There are four methods which are commonly used.

1. *By Oil*. A small greenhouse may be heated by a portable oil apparatus. This will exclude frosts, but a forcing temperature cannot be maintained.

Lamps or stoves with open tops for escape of heat cannot be recommended. The heat is drawn straight up, fumes from the oil can be harmful to the plants, and such heat is apt to produce too dry an atmosphere for many greenhouse plants.

There are firms, however, which have economical and efficient heaters, giving variation of heat according to the weather, and they will burn for three or four days without attention.

2. *By Gas*. A serviceable type of small apparatus is the method of water pipes heated by gas, but so constructed that no fumes can reach the interior of the house.

A typical gas hot water boiler is known as the Shilton. It is constructed for inserting in the end of the house, the lighting door and flue being outside. The gas consumption is economical. By means of the gas regulator provided the gas consumption can be set to suit the piping that has to be heated. Heat can be controlled by regulating the gas tap, also by the use of an automatic temperature regulator. All is automatically controlled and there is no waste.

It is easily fixed, no attention is needed beyond occasional addition of water and the flueways are accessible for cleaning.

No outside construction is needed, thereby saving cost and space.

There is a definite advantage having a gas or oil heater, in that to a great extent they look after themselves, whereas coke and coal apparatus need frequent attention.

3. *By Coke or Coal.* The method of heating generally adopted makes use of a system of hot water pipes heated by a coke boiler installed in the wall or apart from the glasshouse.

There are many modern boilers on the market which are simple, efficient and thoroughly reliable.

The Horse Shoe Boiler is a typical type and is designed to fit in the base of the glasshouse. If required an automatic draught control can be provided at a small extra cost. The ample fuel space ensures heat for long periods without attention. The complete equipment usually includes boiler, expansion tank, flue pipe and hot water pipes, etc., and the installation is usually carried out by an experienced plumber.

The modern boiler has been redesigned to give increased efficiency and strength.

4. *Electrical heating.* The Electrical Tubular system thermostatically controlled is rapidly gaining favour owing to its simplicity of control and lack of attention required.

Much criticism has been levelled at this form of heating owing to the alleged drying of the atmosphere to a greater extent than with the hot-water pipe method. This bogey has definitely been laid in practice and the most highly satisfactory results have been obtainable by this electrical form of heating.

The running cost is on the expensive side but, in the case of the home owner, the extra cost of running is outweighed by the labour saved. A thermostat inserted into the electrical circuit is used to maintain the glasshouse at any pre-determined temperature by cutting off, and switching on, the current when required. This is of great value, being self-operating, as there is no waste in consumption and also the owner is safe-guarded against sudden drops in temperature, as well as too great a forcing heat, at any time.

The layout of piping. It is impossible to give reliable advice on the size of piping required for a given temperature. The advice of the expert must again be resorted to.

The position of pipes should receive careful consideration, making sure that the flow pipes always rise gently from the boiler. The return pipes should have a corresponding fall back to the boiler.

5. *By Oil.* Not as cheap as by coal or Phurnacite – but preferred by some as there is no stoking to do and no ashes to remove.

4 Equipment of the greenhouse

Directly the greenhouse has been built it has to be equipped. Much of the equipment should be incorporated in the building, and the quotation given for the house may include the staging, a sunk water tank, and even a thermometer.

THE STAGING

The side staging should be from 3–4 ft in height, while the central staging may either be of the same height or may be tiered as in the drawing on page 21.

It is convenient, for cleaning purposes, if the surface of the staging is removable. Permanent slatted wood is sometimes used, but it is not ideal, because it gives too great a circulation of air, and plants are apt to dry out in hot weather in consequence.

Slates are therefore sometimes used, and on these, shingle, gravel ash or Lytag, is laid to a depth of 2 in. and this helps to hold the moisture.

Corrugated iron cut to size can be used instead of slates, but this has to be renewed every four or five years because it rusts away. The initial cost of the slates is about five times that of the corrugated iron.

Material on the staging. Shingle is very good indeed, for not only does it last for ever, but it can be washed every year, and if it is going to be used the fine dust should always be sifted out first. If it isn't changed each season it gets very sour, as the result of the continuous waterings and dampings down. Broken shell is another possibility, but is rather white and glaring.

Lytag, sold by John Laing & Sons, is ideal as it is clean, round and doesn't have to be changed each season.

WATER TANK

It is a good plan to sink a tank into the ground at soil level. This can store the rainwater collected from the roof. Rainwater is much better for plants than tap water. A concrete tank

24

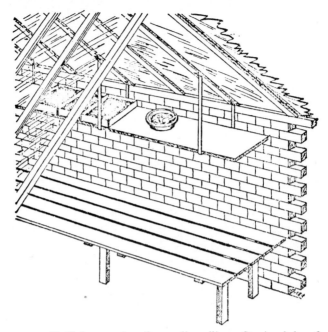

Shelf close to glass for small seedlings. Staging below for established plants

is quite easy to build, and is easier to sterilize and keep clean than a galvanized iron tank.

It is generally convenient to place it underneath the central staging or to one corner of the house. It should be possible to dip the watering cans into it without much effort. Long shallow tanks are therefore preferable to short deep ones.

Should the weather be very dry during the summer and the rainwater in the tank gets low, a tap should be conveniently situated so that the tank may be refilled from the main.

THE PROPAGATING FRAME

A small frame for propagating purposes (see Chapter 7) may easily be made on the staging at the end nearest the boiler. It may consist of a few boards nailed together to form quite a small box or frame, a sheet of glass being placed on the top. It should be filled with coconut fibre refuse, into which the pots and pans of cuttings and seeds can be plunged. This fibre should be kept moist.

Such frames electrically heated can now be had with cloche coverage and are excellent inside a greenhouse.

THE SIEVE

Sieves are necessary for sifting leaves, soil or peat; for the normal greenhouse three sieves should be ample, one $\frac{1}{4}$-in. mesh, one $\frac{1}{2}$-in., and one of mesh 1 in. square. A very fine gauze wire sieve is also useful for sifting sand, or sandy surface soil on to seed pans and boxes.

THE POTTING BRUSH

Circular brushes may be obtained with short handles to fit the pots most commonly used. By their use it is quite easy to clean out the inside of a pot in a very short time.

RAMMERS AND PRESSERS

Ramming sticks of various sizes will help to firm the compost around the outside of the ball when potting. Flat boards with small handles can also be made to fit the various sized boxes, pans and pots, and these are used for obtaining a smooth surface before seed sowing – and for firming.

BAMBOOS AND SUPPORTS

All the supports used in a greenhouse should be as inconspicuous as possible. They should be strong enough to do their work, and yet be slender. Bamboo canes can be bought stained green, and so can specially shaped sticks made for the purpose.

Wire stakes are sometimes used for carnations, begonias and geraniums, and these are fitted with special open ring ends. Special wire erections are sometimes employed up which the trailing and climbing plants are trained.

WIRE FRAMES

Special wire frames may be purchased for the trailing and climbing plants, galvanized rings affixed to galvanized rods may be used for begonias, carnations and the like.

THERMOMETERS AND CHARTS

The thermometer is a most important piece of equipment. It is as well to have a guaranteed tested one, for many of the cheaper kinds on the market are not reliable. If two or three thermometers may be 'borrowed' from the ironmonger and be hung in the greenhouse together the results are often very entertaining!

The man who is really interested in the history of his plants is advised to keep a temperature chart. This can easily be made from any ordinary graph paper, and the actual temperature at say nine o'clock every morning can be plotted on the chart and a graph thus made. It is amazing the difference the careful plotting of a graph can make to the cultivator. He soon knows whether the heating apparatus is doing its job or not, and whether the fuel is being wasted.

THE WATERING CAN

Without a doubt the Haw's patent watering can type is the best for the greenhouse. It has a long spout, and the can may be gripped by the handle or by the crossbar that goes from the opening to the spout. It is, in fact, a perfectly balanced can. It is very easy to dip into the tank, it fills quickly, and the length of spout allows the plants at the back of the staging to be watered easily. The pressure also from the weight of water in the can forces the water out through the finest rose, with perfect evenness.

There are various sizes of these cans; for a large house a 3-gallon can is ideal, and for the moderate sized house the 2-gallon can. For plants on the shelves a Haw's containing 1 gallon is quite sufficient.

A good plastic can is always a good investment. It will outlast the cheaper kind, and because it is properly made is quicker and easier to handle.

THE SYRINGE

Here again it is well worth while investing in a good brass syringe that will last. Syringes are very easily dented, and once they are, the plunger will not move up and down. A syringe made of thin metal will constantly be out of use for this reason.

Some syringes have a particular flange or cup-shaped formation attached to them in order to catch the drips.

For the bigger house two syringes should always be available, the larger one for applying moisture with a good deal of force, i.e. when damping down or washing foliage, and the smaller one for spraying insecticide or fungicide and for watering baby seedlings.

THE POTTING TRAY

Those who have a number of greenhouses build a special potting shed in which the mixing of the composts and the actual potting operations are done. With one greenhouse it is advisable to have a portable potting bench that may be erected on folding legs whenever potting has to be done. This makes it unnecessary to take the young plants out of the house, and so safeguards against their getting chilled.

A convenient potting tray is 2 ft wide, 4 ft long and has back and sides 1 ft high. A smaller sized tray may be made to suit the requirements of the house.

TAPPER

It is quite easy to make a small tapper, which can be fixed at the end of a short or long bamboo as desired. The head of the tapper is normally 1 or $1\frac{1}{2}$ in. in diameter, and $1\frac{1}{2}$ in. long.

5 Managing the greenhouse

Those who are responsible for greenhouse management should always remember that plants should be grown in as natural a way as possible. They should be given atmospheric conditions similar to those which they would experience in their natural habitat. It is a great mistake to coddle, to refuse sufficient air, to overwater or to crowd.

VENTILATION

The ventilators not only help in the regulation of heat but enable fresh air to be supplied. As a general rule it is better to over-ventilate than to under-ventilate. The general theory of air movement, of course, is that the hot air will rise and flow out of the top ventilators, and the cold air will enter to take its place through the side or end ventilators. With a glasshouse this scheme cannot always be relied on, for the inside movement of air is to some extent controlled also by wind movement outside, the position of the sun and so on.

Most houses have top ventilators, in some cases intermittent and in others running the whole length of the house. In addition, there are a certain number of side ventilators and occasionally what are known as bottom ventilators. These are generally of the box type, and are fixed below the staging. They are not found in modern houses because they dry the air around the plants. Gardeners of long ago found them useful in the winter for admitting a little air during the winter when the weather was very frosty.

As a rule the ventilators are opened up early in the morning and are closed down or partially closed down in the afternoon or early evening so as to help trap the sun heat and so save fuel. Naturally the times of opening and closing differ tremendously in summer and winter. It may be necessary to ventilate all night in summer or at any rate not to close the ventilators down until about nine o'clock.

When ventilating always open the top ventilators first, and when they have been letting out hot air for some time then give some side ventilation.

It is necessary to avoid draughts at all costs, and for this reason ventilators should never be opened on the windward side, even if the wind is only a light breeze. Always open side ventilators and top ventilators to leeward.

Ventilation should be given on a rise in temperature; that is why the house is opened up in the morning as the sun begins to rise. There is never any need to get panicky about high temperature if the high temperatures are produced by the sun heat only. There is no harm in the temperature rising 15° if this is due to the sun. A rise of 8° though, due to pipe heat, might be very harmful to the plants. More air is let in to keep the temperature level; the gardener does not primarily give air for the purpose of lowering the temperature.

The 'Extralite' greenhouse showing the ventilator open

To explain it another way, it is necessary to put on air (as it is called) in anticipation of the temperature rising, and not when it actually has risen. In this way the temperature is kept level. A bad gardener gives air when he has too much fire heat. This is not the right way of keeping the temperature down.

The obvious way is to damp down the fire, turn down the gas, reduce the electrical heat, or to regulate whatever method is employed for warming the greenhouse.

Though it may be possible to open the ventilators suddenly, it is *never* advisable to close them down in one movement. The ventilation should be reduced gradually. A little less ventilation as the sun starts to go down, yet a little less, and finally the closing.

The amount of heat used and the time and amount of ventilation given depend very much on weather conditions. During a damp dull period the air in a glasshouse will tend to be sluggish. It is then that greater heat can be used in order to cause the air to circulate and help provide a buoyant atmosphere. This increase in heat should only be done for a short time in the winter, or otherwise weedy growth may result. Naturally, on dull days it is possible to open the ventilators when the house is at a lower temperature than when there are sunny warm periods for the sun heat does not 'injure' plants like pipe heat.

TEMPERATURE

It is difficult to be dictatorial about temperatures for these differ, naturally, from plant to plant. Those who intend to have a cool greenhouse will find it sufficient to have a temperature of round about 50°F during the daytime, and round about 40°F at night time. This during the winter. In the spring, i.e. during April and May the heat may be allowed to be somewhat higher in each case than these figures, say 5° mentioned above to 8° and in the summer very little artificial heat should be required. It is as well just to keep the pipes warm to ensure the circulation of air.

The tendency is to cut off artificial heat altogether – and although this can be done the air in the glasshouse will become stagnant, and mildews and other fungi thrive in consequence.

Those who go in for plants that like a warmer atmosphere should aim at a temperature of 45°F at night and 55°F in the day during the autumn and winter, and say 55°F at night time and 65°F in the daytime in the spring and summer.

The man with one small greenhouse who wishes to grow a variety of plants will naturally have to try and strike the happy medium. Fortunately, it is extraordinary the way that plants will get accustomed to, and grow quite well in, temperatures at which they are supposed not to thrive. As a general rule it is better to err on the lower side where heat is concerned, though every precaution should be taken to keep out frost during the winter.

SHADING

Another method of keeping down the temperature is to use some form of shading. Plants that are growing in full sun are apt to dry out very quickly and shading or partial shading naturally prevents this. Plants need damping down or syringing when growing under glass and they may be scorched as a result if the house is not shaded. This, of course, also reduces the temperature.

Many plants, like ferns and the primulas, do best in shade and if they do not have it they wilt.

There is no need to shade unless the sun is strong. Shading which is done during a dull summer or when the sun is quite mild can be harmful, for the leaves of the plants will be unable to manufacture elaborated sap, with the result that the growth will be both leggy and weak.

Shading can be done in various ways. Some like to use flour and water, and this has the advantage of being able to be put on thinly. It is not, however, good either for the putty or for the paintwork and so its use cannot be advised.

A solution of garden lime in water or whitewash is very common and can be sprayed or put on with the lime wash brush. There is a tendency to put it on too thickly, and care should be taken to prevent this.

There is a special shading known as Verishade which goes on quite clear in rainy damp weather and appears opaque in sunny periods.

Some horticultural sundriesmen sell a special greenish wash for the purpose commonly known as Summer Cloud. This is easy to apply, lasts well and gives just the right shade desired. Unfortunately, it is quite expensive.

The ideal is to use blinds, made either of slatted wood or green plastic material. These can be raised or lowered as desired and can be used one side of the house or the other as necessary. They not only give protection against sun heat during the summer, but they can act, if it is desired, as an extra guard against frost during a cold winter's night. Plastic blinds naturally are better taken down during the winter and stored to prevent them from rotting, but the slatted wooden blinds can remain on their rollers at the head of the glasshouse all year round.

WATERING

One of the most difficult things to teach students at the Arkley Horticultural College is correct watering. The true plant lover gets to know by experience whether it is right to water or whether moisture should be withheld. It is possible to tell almost by looking at a plant and by knowing it, too, of course, whether it ought to be watered.

There are, however, some general principles to be followed and these will be dealt with.

First of all the natural habitat of the plant must be known. Does it normally grow in the desert or on boggy land? Is it found in nature on the tops of mountains or in the valleys? Does it grow best on a northern or southern slope if left to nature?

Naturally, the conditions in the glasshouse cannot be exactly the same, but plants from desert regions will require little water, and this should perhaps be given in the spring when the moisture will be stored in the leaves as in the case of Euphorbias which come from Madagascar. Where plants come from districts where the rains are seasonal and where there are periods of long drought, the plants in the greenhouse should have a similar dry resting period. The greenhouse owner gives this opportunity by placing the plants under the staging and leaving them there until their period of growth and watering comes round again. This is the way to treat Thunias from India, and Gloxinias which come to us from Brazil. Plants should not be dried out suddenly, nor should they be watered again just as suddenly. Both the drying off process and the bringing into growth process should be done gradually.

Where little is known about the plant's history much can be learnt from the look of the plant. If it has a woody stem with tiny leaves like the heaths, little water may be necessary, but the plant should never be allowed to dry out; if the leaves are thick and leathery then it is a type of succulent and in all probability comes from droughty conditions so that watering need not be so frequent.

The plants that have large and broad leaves and are quick growing will require watering almost every day, but the plants with more leathery leaves that grow slowly will appreciate being syringed over and will not require so much moisture at the roots.

There are other factors that affect watering. When a plant is growing and is manufacturing plant food it needs plenty of water, for this helps in conveying the elaborated plant food from the leaves to other parts of the plant. When, on the other hand, the plants start to flower they are using up the manufactured food and so need less water. As a matter of fact plants that are given heavy waterings when in flower usually cease flowering promptly, as may be proved by treating annuals out of doors in this manner.

In the winter plants are never as active as during the spring and summer, and so, even if they are not resting, the amount of water supplied may be reduced. Again, during bright sunny periods more water is required than during dull weather. The greater the ventilation the more quickly will plants dry out, and this is one of the reasons why in sunny weather shading should be given in addition to ventilation.

Old plants, like geraniums, that have been cut back will need far less water because the leaf surface has been reduced and yet the root system remains the same. Plants that are really healthy need more moisture at their roots than those that are sickly. Where plants are pot bound more water has to be applied than where there is plenty of soil in which the root system can grow.

The amount of water given also depends on the soil. A good peaty compost requires less watering than one that is rich in sand (this is one of the reasons that the use of sedge peat is recommended in Chapter 6). A peaty compost should never be allowed to dry out though, and if it does the pot should be well soaked in a tub and not watered in the ordinary way. (There are special composts which need less water, see Chapter 6.)

A plant that is potted firmly always requires less water than a similar plant potted loosely.

Flagging may be caused both by under-watering or by over-watering. As a rule when too little water is given, the plants stop growing and start to harden, while the lower leaves will fall off. If too much water is given the compost becomes airless, the leaves go yellow and the plant looks sick and eventually dies.

The water should always be at the same temperature as the house and soft water is better than hard water. It is advisable to use a rose on a watering can, especially with newly potted plants. A good general rule is never to direct water over the crown of the plant in the case of those that tend to rot at the crown, e.g. primulas. In this case watering should not be done with the rose, and the gardener's finger can direct the water flow if placed over the end of the spout.

It is a mistake to give little sprinklings of water continually. Watering should always be done thoroughly when it is done, and if possible just before the plant requires it. It is quite a good idea to tap the pot with a little wooden hammer or with the knuckles and by the sound which is heard a good gardener can tell whether water is necessary or not. The clear hollow ringing tone of the clay pot means the plant needs watering. A rather dull low muffled tone means that the soil is sufficiently moist. This tapping is useless in the case of plastic pots.

The modern plastic pots need far less watering than do the clay pots, because the clay evaporates a great deal of the moisture, whereas the plastic pots do not.

In summer it is better to water in the evening so as to give the plants a chance of using the moisture during the cool period. This doesn't mean that it isn't possible to water plants

Two primulas grown at the same time, one in a clay pot the other in a plastic pot. Evaporation from the sides of the clay has kept the soil colder

in sunlight. In the winter it is best to water about ten o'clock in the morning as from this time onwards the temperature should begin to rise. As a result the surplus water will drain away before nightfall.

Pans and shallow boxes of seedlings are best watered by standing them in a shallow container filled with water at the right temperature. Overhead watering tends to encourage damping off. To avoid continual watering, some gardeners plunge such pans and boxes into peat moss or fibre.

DAMPING DOWN

Damping down or syringing should be used as an adjunct to watering and is most important in the warmer greenhouses where moist conditions are necessary. It prevents plants from transpiring too much, helps to keep the atmosphere moist and does much to control red spider and thrips, particularly the former.

The actual damping is done to the paths, staging, pipes and walls. It can be done with a coarse syringe or through the spout of a watering can.

Fine syringing is done to provide a kind of natural dew or rain. It helps to prevent flagging, and to keep the leaves fresh and clean. It is always best to syringe the underside of leaves first and then to give them a light sprinkling over. One syringing a day is usually sufficient during the winter, and four syringings may be necessary in a warm summer. A plant in flower, a hairy-leaved plant, or an inactive plant should never be syringed.

CLEANLINESS

It seems hardly necessary to emphasize the necessity for cleanliness. If it is advisable in the garden, it is all the more important under glass.

Dead leaves and flowers should always be picked off and burnt, the pots should be weeded regularly, and moss and algae should never be allowed to accumulate on the top of pots, as this prevents air from getting at the roots. The sides of pots should also be kept clean, particularly in the case of epiphytal orchids. Evergreen plants should have their leaves syringed, and if necessary sponged, to prevent dust collecting on them. All inside walls should be whitewashed at least once a year, and where there are inside tanks these should be cleaned out regularly, the insides being scrubbed well, and painted with a thin Portland cement wash, or if this is not readily available, with whitewash, as this will assist in reducing corrosion.

The outside of the glass should be cleaned at least once a year, and those who live in sooty towns will be advised to wash the outside with a detergent three or four times a year. Where the panes have got really engrimed Premax acid should be used, and be washed off immediately. This will clean up the dirtiest glass.

The inside of the house should be washed once a year with carbolic soft soap to which 6 fl. oz of formaldehyde have been added to 2 gallons of water. It is easiest to wash during the mid summer as many of the plants can then be put outside.

Paint the outside of the house with genuine white lead paint at least every three years. The inside of the house should also be similarly painted every three years. This is the minimum life which would be expected from genuine white lead paint, and it may be found that the paint is in good condition for an appreciably longer period, in which case the maintenance period could be lengthened. It is important that the paint should be applied when the surface is free from moisture and for this reason outside painting during unfavourable weather conditions, such as when it is raining, foggy or in the early morning after a frost, should be avoided.

For the painting of houses with high temperature and humidity conditions, some authorities prefer the use of white lead-zinc oxide mixtures, where the zinc oxide does not exceed 25 per cent of the total pigment. Special greenhouse paints of this type are available ready mixed from leading white lead paint manufacturers.

Some people like to paint the pipes and generally use for the purpose a good vegetable black mixed with boiled linseed oil and turpentine, and a little paste drier. The reason for using this paint material is to obtain a black surface which is the most effective for the radiation of heat. However, if it is borne in mind that the heating pipes in a glasshouse work to a greater extent by heat convection which is not affected by the colour of the surface, rather than by heat radiation and also that there is only a small percentage difference in the radiation value for different surfaces, it will be appreciated that this special treatment is not nearly so important as it might at first be considered.

It might be better practice to paint the pipes with white

lead in with the rest of the work, and get the maximum of *reflected* light possible, as well as good protection against corrosion of the pipes.

Where shingle is used on the staging this should be removed once a year, be washed in suitable sieves and replaced. Where Lytag is used it can remain in position for several years.

It is not possible to be too careful about cleanliness in a glasshouse, for it is so easy to harbour pests and diseases in all sorts of cracks and crannies.

6 Composts and potting

The whole question of composts was revolutionized as the result of the work of Messrs. W. J. C. Lawrence and J. Newell at the John Innes Horticultural Institution, Merton. They pointed out that there was no need for the fifty or so different composts that gardeners had to remember in the olden days, and that for the majority of plants two composts should be quite sufficient.

JOHN INNES COMPOSTS
The principles they laid down were briefly as follows:
(1) The compost must be in the right physical condition, be free from harmful organisms, and provide an adequate, balanced food supply.
(2) That the compost should be sterilized by heating it to a minimum temperature of 180°F for 30 minutes.
(3) That the fertilizers should be added in the right proportion both in the case of seed sowing and of potting.
(4) That the compost should contain loam, sedge peat and sand in the right proportions.
(5) That the ingredients of the compost should be partially sterilized separately, and then be mixed afterwards and the fertilizers added.
(6) That the strictest hygiene should be practised in all matters.
   The two composts recommended were:

Compost No. 1. John Innes Seed Compost: 2 parts by bulk medium loam; 1 part by bulk good sedge peat; 1 part by bulk coarse sand; adding to each bushel of this mixture $1\frac{1}{2}$ oz superphosphate of lime and 1 oz ground limestone or chalk.

Compost No. 2. John Innes Potting Compost: 7 parts by bulk medium loam; 3 parts by bulk good sedge peat; 2 parts by bulk coarse sand; adding to each bushel of this mixture $1\frac{1}{2}$ oz hoof and horn meal, $\frac{1}{8}$ in. grist, $1\frac{1}{2}$ oz superphosphate of lime, $\frac{3}{4}$ oz sulphate of potash and 1 oz ground limestone or chalk. A bushel of soil will exactly fill a box measuring 22 in. × 10 in. × 10 in.

It should be pointed out that it always proved better to sift the superphosphate and sulphate of potash through a 1/16 in. sieve before making up the mixture, or before adding the fertilizers to the compost. Readers should not try to vary the proportions of the fertilizers on their own account; they should be strictly adhered to, and not merely approximated, but be weighed carefully.

The same rule applies when measuring the soil. A wheelbarrow of a known capacity should be used, or a biscuit tin, the main thing being to make certain that the quantities are correct.

The potting compost may be used for pricking off for the majority of the plants.

It does not seem to matter very much the quality of the loam used, provided the fertilizers have been added and the compost is in the right physical condition. Good garden soil 'seems' just as effective as an expensive loam.

Though sterilization has been advised, it is not always necessary to treat the sand if it is clean and free from weeds, lime and organic matter. If a good horticultural sedge peat is used, there is no need to sterilize this either.

When soil is sterilized it should be riddled first of all so that it is broken down into small pieces. Passed through a $\frac{1}{2}$-in. sieve it is in the right condition, and will mix well with the fertilizers.

Only fair results may be had using the J.I. formulae when the soil has not been sterilized.

The temperature of the soil should always be measured with a thermometer and never guessed and after sterilizing is over, the hot soil should be removed immediately, and be spread out to allow excess moisture to evaporate.

It is inadvisable to store a sterilized compost for more than two months, though the separate ingredients may be kept after sterilizing for much longer.

The strictest hygiene should be practised under glass. It isn't much use being particular about sterilized soil and then being careless about hygiene in other directions.

ALEXPEAT COMPOSTS

Alex composts, as a whole, contain special quality peat, which is conditioned, selected, blended, screened and graded to give the required aeration and water holding capacity. The sedge peats used have a high humus content, being twice as dense as sphagnum peat giving a greater natural organic buffering action helpful against variations in feeding levels. The seven types of composts prepared by Alexanders of Burnham-on-Sea, Somerset, have various nutrient levels to meet the requirements of a range of crops. All the composts contain a wetting agent which normalizes watering techniques, and eliminates the problem of rewetting an over dry peat compost.

The only other special composts that should be necessary are those for orchids, not dealt with here, but to which it is hoped to devote a future book in the series.

Terrestrial orchids. 1 part fibrous loam, 1 part orchid peat, 1 part sphagnum moss, 1 part old cow manure, $\frac{1}{2}$ parts sand, brick dust, charcoal.

Epiphytal orchids. 1 part osmunda fibre, 1 part sphagnum moss, 1/32 part of charcoal.

POT PREPARATION

New clay pots should always be soaked before use, otherwise they absorb the moisture from the soil. Old clay pots should be thoroughly washed so as to ensure that they are porous and clean.

Crocking is necessary for drainage, and each pot should have one large crock put over the drainage hole, concave side downwards. Composts of sandy proportions need less crocking than perennials, plants that are going to be potted on require less crocks than plants that are being transferred into their final pots. Plastic pots do not need crocking.

POTTING OFF, UP, ON, ETC.

The term potting on indicates the moving of a plant from a small pot to a larger one. The term potting up or off is used when seedlings or cuttings are potted from seed trays.

Repotting is the shaking out of soil from the old ball and potting it back into the same sized pot. Potting back refers to the knocking out of a plant, rubbing off the shoulders and sides of the ball and putting into a smaller pot.

Rooted cuttings should be potted up when the roots are about $\frac{1}{2}$ in. long. If you leave them longer, they are apt to be damaged by handling.

SHIFTING SIZES

Plants should never be allowed to become pot bound until they are in the pot where they are to flower.

The size of shift naturally varies according to the plant. Quick growers will stand a larger shift better than slow growers. An inch difference is usually allowed in a pot, the rule being to pot on gradually.

A smaller shift should be given when potting in the autumn than in the spring. The ball of the plant that is going to be potted should be moist, and the shape of the ball may be squeezed into that of a rugby football. This facilitates correct watering in the new pot. The compost should always be at the same temperature as the house from which the plants have come, and the old ball should never be buried in the new compost. It should not, either, appear over the top of the new compost, but should be exactly level.

The physical condition of the soil is a great factor in potting, and though firm potting is essential, ramming is to be deprecated. When potting on, the soil around the ball of a plant grown in a 60 and potted in a 48 pot must be harder than the 60's ball. If this is not done the plant ball will get dry in the middle, and once the original ball does get dry in a 5 in. pot it is almost impossible to get it wet again, and so the plant will not thrive.

Plants that have been in pots for some time, and are to be repotted into a similar sized pot should have the soil shaken off their roots, and the compost No. 2 made up for them. Care should be taken when potting not to allow the roots to get into a 'huddle' – always spread them out.

SUBSTANCES USED IN POTTING

Leaf mould. The best is made from oak and beech leaves because of their small veins. The leaves should be collected in the autumn and be stacked. They should be turned two or three times a year and they are then ready in two years time when they pass easily through a $\frac{1}{2}$ in. sieve.

Sedge peat. This peat that has been specially treated is useful because it holds the moisture and when supplied, is free from diseases and pests and weed seeds. It is rich in humus.

Sand. Silver sand should always be used of a fairly coarse texture, sand that is too fine cakes and so is useless and red sand has iron in it and also sets hard.

Sea sand is a possibility, but it has to be washed again and again, and then be left for a year to weather. The great value of sand is in the way it opens up a compost and supplies air. It is used greatly in the propagation of cuttings for this reason.

Crushed brick or crocks. Crushed brick or crocks are sometimes used to supplement sand. This has the advantage of absorbing the moisture and does not dry out.

Coconut fibre refuse. Used for striking cuttings in a propagating case, and for growing bulbs in bowls.

Mortar rubble. Useful in opening up the soil and for the purpose of adding lime – often for chrysanthemums.

Soot. Sprinkles are sometimes given to pots in order to give depth of colour to leaves, especially valuable in the case of foliage plants, must be kept dry, and not be used until it has been stored for four months.

Wood ashes. Contain a small quantity of potash, sometimes added to the compost if the garden soil used is heavy, must be given dry.

Sphagnum moss. Used for lining hanging baskets. As long as the moss looks green the basket does not require watering. This is a good indicator. It is the only moss that will 'live' out of the soil. It should be kept damp in a bag. Sometimes used for orchids.

Polypodium fibre. Used for seedling orchids.

Osmunda fibre. Used for orchids. More expensive than Polypodium.

Fertilizers and top dressings. Fertilizers may be added to pot plants, preferably in the form of a balanced plant food with an organic base, such as a good fish manure. This may be sprinkled on the soil at the rate of a pinch for 3-in. pots, a teaspoonful for 5-in., increasing the amount per size of pot and requirement of plants. Water in with a can with a rose.

Owing to constant watering, the soil is often washed away from the plant roots, so it is advisable to top dress each pot with Alex Soil-less Compost No. 2. Never feed or top dress a dry plant.

LIQUID MANURES
The practice of giving cow manure water has now been dispensed with in favour of liquid manure which gives more certain results.

Lately liquid manures organic in their origin have been made available to the public in bottles. These concentrated liquids have a guaranteed analysis and can be used with success in the greenhouse once diluted in accordance with the instructions on the label.

Most gardeners prefer to use Farmura or Maxicrop as this gives the plant regular feeds of easily available foods.

The Horticultural Training College, which recommends these liquid fertilizers, has used them on plants for four months without a break except for weekends, with excellent results.

In the case of big plants or large numbers of plants crowded in boxes a stronger solution can be used quite safely periodically.

Even quite small plants may be watered all over with this 'feed' provided the plants immediately after a wetting are not exposed to strong sunlight.

EQUIPMENT

CLAY POTS

Normal flower pots are made of earthenware and are left unglazed. Latterly some glass pots have been put on to the market, but these are at the present time more expensive. Cardboard, bituminized, and prepared peat pots are also available. These do not last long, but have the advantage of disintegrating when put into the soil, so transplanting may be

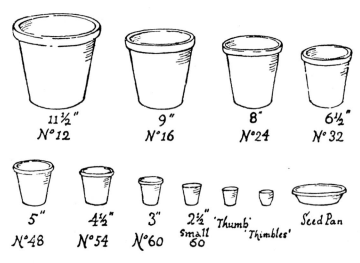

Flower pots showing sizes and numbers used in the trade

done without root disturbance. Earthenware pots are sold by the cast, so many pots to a cast. The term 60's or 48's refers to the number of pots in a cast.

A COMPARISON OF CLAY POTS AND PLASTIC POTS

The advantages of the plastic pots are:

(1) They are light in weight.
(2) There is virtually no breakage.
(3) They are easy to store – the Close Nesting Rim Design facilitates large savings in storage space.
(4) They can be steam sterilized if necessary.
(5) They are easier to transport due to their lightness and durability.

7 Propagation

The glasshouse gives unusual opportunities for all kinds of methods of propagation. Owing to the varied number and types of plants grown under glass it is necessary to understand the methods of propagation best suited to the individual plant. Naturally, in some cases it is possible to propagate one plant by various ways, and the gardener has then to decide which method suits his particular purpose best.

PROPAGATION BY SEED

When plants can be propagated by seed a stronger root system develops, for the plant grows naturally. Seed sowing is used to regenerate old stock, for by continuous vegetative propagation plants tend to degenerate e.g. cinerarias, or may be more prone to diseases, e.g. hollyhocks, which suffer from rust.

Seed sowing helps also with the housing problem for the youngsters can often be raised in frames or under cloches and can be taken into the greenhouse later.

Some plants, particularly conifers, are more shapely when grown from seed.

The disadvantage of seed sowing is that many plants do not come true from seed. This either means true to colour or true to type. Other plants do not flower as quickly, and in this case vegetative propagation is obviously to be preferred, because it gives you an extra year or two of flowering.

CARE OF SEEDS AND TIME OF SOWING

Seeds should always be stored under the best possible conditions. The tiny seeds should be kept in non-absorbent paper bags, and in a dry cupboard at a temperature of 40–45°F. Some seeds with a high water content should be kept in moss, viz. maple and chestnut, while water lily seeds need storing in water. Hard coated seeds like nuts are usually kept in sand outside so that they can be frozen, to ensure that they split. The rose and holly seeds should be kept for a year in this way before being sown.

Other seeds need special treatment. The hard coated black

skin of sweet pea seeds needs a slight filing or nicking. Acacia seeds should be heated over the fire or dropped for a few moments in boiling water. The seed of the asparagus fern should be put into warm water for twenty-four hours and should then be sown immediately afterwards.

Most of the hardy annuals can be sown outside in the autumn or in March. The half-hardy annuals are sown in the greenhouse in late February, in frames in March, or in the open in April and early May. Most of the greenhouse plants may be raised by seed sowing in February and March. The exceptions are perhaps primulas and cinerarias which should be sown as soon as they can be obtained.

With trees and shrubs the seed sowing periods may be at two periods: the exotic types need sowing in late February or March so as to ensure that the seedlings appear when the weather is likely to be favourable; those indigenous to this country should have their seeds sown as soon as they mature.

VARIOUS METHODS OF SEED SOWING

The general rules with regard to seed sowing are drawn from Nature. A seed like the chestnut which falls before the leaves thus obtains a good covering of leaf mould. Smaller seeds usually fall with the leaves so that they are not covered so deeply.

This shows the use of organic matter, and that the seeds only need covering three times their own width.

Naturally, seeds may be sown in light soils and in light composts deeper than in heavy soils. Seeds in pans are often not covered at all, or just have the slightest quantity of sandy compost sifted over through a fine sieve.

A good standard compost for seed sowing will be found in Chapter 6. For the larger seeds the compost may go through a $\frac{1}{4}$-in. sieve and for the smaller seeds through a 1/16-in. sieve. Good drainage must be ensured, and the top of the soil should be made firm. The compost should nearly reach the top of the pan or box so as to prevent the young seedlings from becoming drawn when they start to grow. It is a good idea when sowing very fine black seed to sprinkle a little white sand on the top of the box or pan, as this enables the gardener to sow sufficiently thinly. Another good plan is to mix fine seed with fine sand and sow the two together. This helps with even distribution. With such seed it is usually better to water the box or pan before sowing.

After sowing and/or watering the pan or box should be covered with a sheet of glass and then a sheet of newspaper. The glass prevents the compost from drying out too quickly and the darkness encourages root formation. Primulas, however, prefer light.

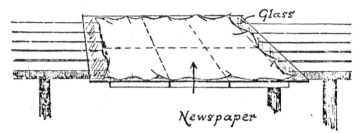

After sowing seeds the boxes are covered with glass and newspaper

With very expensive seeds the pan should be plunged in moss, the latter being watered and not the pan. A sprinkling of sand occasionally on the surface will keep away algae, and this is especially necessary when the seeds are slow germinators.

SAVING YOUR OWN SEED

Save the seed on a fine dry day, be sure that the seed is just ripe and only save from plants of a pure strain. Leave the seeds in a saucer to dry in the sun unless it is known that they have a high water content. When collecting large quantities hang the seeding heads upside down in dry paper bags.

Some seeds lose vitality quickly and so should be sown almost immediately, e.g. cineraria, delphinium and aquilegia, other seeds like cucumbers will keep for years. The seeds of the magnolia and willow often begin to germinate on the plant.

SOWING SPORES

Ferns are raised from spores. These have got to be caught at the right time, that is just before they burst from their sporangia. The fronds should be cut off and be placed between two pieces of smooth paper for storage, and then kept in a warm, dry atmosphere.

The compost used should be similar to that employed for the adults, but it should be passed through a very fine sieve, the top being even finer. It should be sterilized, and this can be done by covering with a sheet of brown paper and then pouring boiling water over. A sheet of glass should cover until cool, and then the spores may be sown and covered with glass again.

As ferns like moisture the house should be kept on the damp side during propagation. Light is necessary, but not strong sun.

When one or two young fronds appear the ferns may be pricked out and be kept moist. Spore sowing may be carried out at any time of the year when the spores are ripe, but a sowing early in the year is usually best.

VEGETATIVE PROPAGATION

Plants propagated in this way are true to type, but more prone to disease. It is possible, though, to produce large numbers quickly.

DIVISION

The simplest method perhaps is division which can be done in spring or autumn. The time actually depends on the condition of the plant, and it is sometimes advisable to work on a little soil into the centre of the clump chosen for propagation some weeks before dividing in order to encourage new growth. The outside portions of the clump are the youngest parts and so are the most vigorous.

LAYERING

By layering, plants are induced to produce roots artificially. It is only possible to raise a limited number of plants from one parent, though with serpentine layering a greater number results. Part of the plant needs burying. The layer usually strikes more easily if it is partially severed at a node and if it is pegged down into a compost containing peat and sand. Serpentine layering is used principally for clematis and wistaria.

SUCKERS

Suckers sometimes come up from the parent plants quite naturally, and these may then be severed and potted up on their own.

CUTTINGS

All kinds of cuttings may be taken, e.g. hard wood, half-ripe, soft and root. Those taken in the winter do not grow as well as those taken in the summer. An open compost should be used, that is one containing plenty of sand. It should be slightly acid, and may be watered with advantage with white vinegar in water. Three teaspoons of this vinegar are sufficient for a gallon

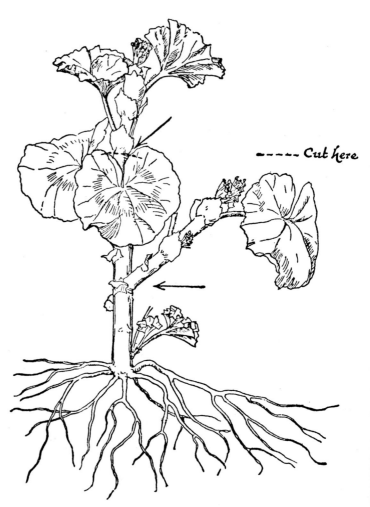

----- Cut here

Plant showing from where cuttings may be taken

of water. The atmosphere for cuttings should be close to prevent transpiration and the base should always rest firmly on soil. It is useless to make holes with a dibber, and then insert the cutting so that it is hanging, as it were, in mid air.

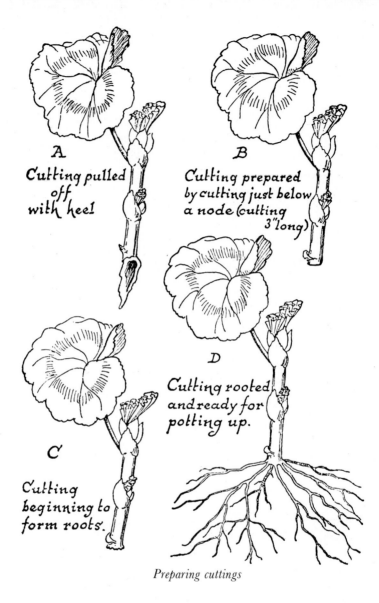

Preparing cuttings

Hormones. Recent experimental work has shown that certain substances stimulate plant growth, and in the case of cuttings, preparations are now obtainable into which the ends are dipped and resulting in a good root system being speedily developed.

Cuttings should only be taken from healthy plants, and

should not be too large or too small. The cuts should be made with the sharp blade of a knife, straight and clean.

Hardwood cuttings. These are generally taken from shrubby plants in October. They may be no longer than 8 or 9 in. long and should be removed with a small heel. They can usually be struck outside and may be placed in a narrow trench with a sanded bottom. The cuttings should be put in 2 in. apart, the soil put back, and packed firmly. If the tips are soft they should be pinched out, otherwise the frost may kill them.

Half-ripe cuttings. These are usually removed and struck during the months of June, July, August and September. They are taken when the wood starts to ripen, and the gardener's test is as follows: the shoot should be bent, and if it snaps and is left hanging by a skin then it is ripe. Such cuttings are struck in a frame on the north side of the garden, or even around the edge of a pot in a shaded frame.

Soft cuttings. These are taken in June and July and will root quickly in pure sand in a heated frame. A Paris frame is sometimes used, that is, a frame containing nothing but pure silver sand placed over perfect drainage. The frame should be placed so that it receives the whole sun. The cuttings are just pushed into the sand, watered regularly, sometimes once an hour. There is no need for the frame to be heated, the sun should supply this.

GREENHOUSE CUTTINGS

Cuttings in the greenhouse itself may be taken either in the autumn or in the spring. The plants that are grown in cool conditions can be propagated by cuttings struck in sand in a miniature frame on the staging. The plants that need a higher temperature are propagated in a frame at a higher temperature too. The baby frame or propagating case as it is called, should have bottom heat and should be filled with peat moss which will hold the moisture.

The cuttings should be struck around the edge of a pot containing a compost consisting of one part loam, one part finely divided leaf-mould and one part sand. A little sand should be sprinkled on top of the compost in addition so that when the hole is made for the cutting the sand is taken to the bottom.

Cuttings should never be struck deeper than is necessary just to hold them upright.

Special exceptions. Conifers and plants that are filled with resin are difficult to strike. Once the cuttings are severed from their parents they should be dipped into boiling water to prevent the resin from forming. It is always better with conifers to take the top shoot.

Some plants contain camphor, oils and alkaloids, and in this case the plants should be stood in the dark for twenty days before being severed from their parents.

The plants with plenty of pith should be cut back, some time before the cuttings are required, and the new side growths should be chosen for propagating.

ROOT CUTTINGS

Any plant that has thick roots may be propagated in this way. Portions of root should be chosen 1 to 2 in. long, the part of the root nearest the stem being planted uppermost. The top of the cutting is usually cut level, and the bottom to a point. They should be buried in a light compost so that the top is covered to a depth of $\frac{1}{2}$ in.

LEAF CUTTINGS

Most plants can be propagated by their leaves, unless the latter are very thin. Propagating from leaves is useful in the case of rare plants, and saves removing shoots; leaves from the lower part of the plant should be chosen.

With begonias the veins of the leaf should be cut through without penetrating the other side. It should then be placed on peat moss litter with plenty of bottom heat, and roots and young plants will appear at the cut places.

In the case of the Saint Paulia, corms are formed at the end of the petiole or stalk provided this is not buried too deeply. In this case the leaf should be placed on its edge in the peat moss litter.

With lilies, the leaf scales are used in October, these being placed in a leafy compost up to the tip, while with the lachenalia corms appear in eight weeks' time if the leaves are placed in a compost and the plants thus raised will flower in two years' time.

BULBS AND CORMS

Various bulbs produce offsets, either naturally or artificially. The centre bud is sometimes destroyed by means of a pointed stick in order that other bulblets will form around.

Some plants like lilies produce bulbils on their stems, and these may be taken off and placed apex upwards in a leafy compost.

Gladioli have tiny corms at the base of the parent, and these may be grown on and will make big plants.

Some plants have what are known as pseudo-bulbs, for instance orchids and thunias, and the long stems of the latter, when in a dormant condition, may be cut up into lengths 4 in. long and placed in a propagating case as advised for warm houses, and as a result they will grow.

TUBERS

Plants having tuberous roots like begonias may be cut into pieces provided each one has an eye. Tuberous begonias are a typical example.

BUDDING

Some plants do not do well on their own roots or do better on the roots of other plants. This operation is carried out in July or August. A slit $1\frac{1}{2}$ in. long should be made in one-year-old wood with a right-angled cut $\frac{1}{2}$ in. long at the top.

The buds chosen should be firm, and be from the current year's growth. They should be removed with the sharp blade of a knife so as not to make a deep incision. The bud may then be inserted the right way up in the T-shaped cut whose bark has been slightly raised for the purpose. The bud should be bound with bass from the bottom upwards, the actual 'nose' of the bud being allowed to peep out. The binding should be loosened in three weeks. If the leak stalks drop off naturally, the bud has 'taken', but if it withers it has not.

In March the stock should be cut down to within 3 or 4 in. above the bud, and as the bud grows it should be tied in loosely to this 'snag'. The following June, the stock may be cut back still further to a point just above the bud.

GRAFTING

Grafting may be done both under glass and outside. Under glass it is usually carried out in February or March, or even in July, August and September. Outside grafting time is usually April and May.

In all cases the stock and scion must be in the same condition. It is usual to remove the scions (pieces of one-year-old wood) in the winter and to heel them in sand outside.

Whip and tongue grafting is carried out when the stock and scion are of the same size; saddle grafting when the stock is somewhat larger than the scion, while root grafting is done under glass when the plant is dormant, in a similar manner to whip and tongue grafting. In this case the graft is covered with soil and placed in a propagating case with a certain amount of bottom heat.

8 Vegetables under glass

A glasshouse can be used for growing large numbers of vegetables. There seems no reason to suppose that all vegetables could not be grown under glass if necessity arose. As a general rule, however, in this country the glasshouse is only used for those vegetables that do not grow as profitably or succulently out of doors, or for the growing of vegetables so as to get them out of season.

This chapter will therefore deal briefly with such crops, but mentions also various vegetables which are raised in the greenhouse ready for planting out later on.

Tomatoes

General. It is said that the tomato was first mentioned in literature in 1554. It certainly appeared in a book called *The History of Plants* published in 1557 where it was called Le Pomme D'Or. It was not popular as a vegetable until about 1882 when it was sold in the London markets. Now tomato growing is an industry of great magnitude.

Heavy crops of tomatoes have been produced from plants growing in only 6 in. of soil, but normally they prefer a good depth of earth, adequate drainage and plenty of head room. Tomato growing as such usually covers a full season, i.e. the sowing done in December and January – the planting in February and March – the picking from the end of April until October. Sometimes tomatoes are used as a catchcrop in the greenhouse, for instance from February till early July. It is possible also to have a crop from a planting made at the end of July and to continue on until the middle of December. Another interesting method is to pot up young plants into 8 or 9 in. pots in July, grow the plants outside until the middle of September, and then take them indoors to continue the fruiting there.

Propagation. The greatest care should be taken in raising the seedlings. The compost, the boxes, the pots and even the staging must be free from pests and diseases. Some Alex

Soil-less Compost should be placed in the glasshouse some days
before it is required so that it is warmed through. The boxes
are then filled with a compost in such a manner that the soil is
of the same firmness throughout so that the moisture-holding
capacity is even. Great care should be taken to firm around
the edges and corners. Fill to within $\frac{3}{4}$ in. of the top of the
boxes, firm well and sift another $\frac{1}{4}$ in. of the compost on the
top, through a piece of perforated zinc, fixed on to the sides
of a box instead of the bottom, and thus used as a sieve.

The box or boxes will then need watering and when
sufficient water has drained away sowing may be done. It is
usual to space the seeds out at 1 in. intervals each way. Some
gardners use a piece of perforated metal cut to fit the inside
of the seed tray exactly, and drilled with the right number of
holes of sufficiently large diameter to allow the seeds to be
pushed through. This is the quickest way of tackling the job.

The slightest film of compost should then be sifted over the
seeds and a further firming given with a firming board – just
lightly. Cover each box with a sheet of glass and over the top
of this a piece of brown paper and each morning turn the glass
upside down and put the paper back. The accumulated
moisture on the underside is thus dried out. Continue this
procedure till the seedlings appear and then remove the glass,
leaving the paper on for another day or two. During the
whole of this period the temperature of the house should not
go below 60°F. Keep the atmosphere of the house moist and
buoyant, so damp down the pathways and the soil beneath
the staging and so on every day. The only exceptions are
during a very cold dull period when the seedlings should be
kept on the dry side.

Potting up. When the first two real leaves have developed the
plants may be potted up into 3-in. pots, using the Alex
Soil-less Compost or No. 2 John Innes compost. Crocks are
usually not placed in the bottom of the pot, but instead a
small quantity of coarser bits of compost are put into position
first and the rest of the specially mixed soil is put on the top.
Care must be taken not to pinch the stems of the plants with
the fingers. They should always be held by the leaves. A
seedling can be held with one hand and the pot filled with soil
with the other. Once the plant is upright both hands can be
used for firming the soil in the pot and thus all avoidance of
injury to seedlings is ensured. Do not pot tightly as during
watering the soil is bound to become tighter. Always leave

Tomato seedling ready for first potting

about $\frac{1}{4}$ in. of space at the top of the pot for watering. See that the plant is in the centre of the pot with the seed leaves resting on the soil. Be sure the surface of the soil is level and that no finger or thumb marks can be seen.

After potting. Stand the potted seedlings on the staging. Water well through the fine rose of a can and keep the temperature of the house at 65°F at night-time with a slight rise by day, so as to help the plants to get over their disturbance. More damping down of the pathways and pipes will be necessary. Directly the plants become established reduce the temperature to 60°F and on all favourable days give some ventilation, even if only for an hour or so in the middle of the day. Water as little as possible though, it is better to keep the plants on the dry side. Aim at a sticky sturdy plant with a good root system. Watch out for what are called rogues. These are deformed dwarf plants very often with fern-like leaves or the spaces between the leaves being reduced so that the plants give the appearance of a rosette. These 'Jacks' or 'Christmas trees' as they are sometimes called, must be discarded promptly.

Planting. When the plants are 5 or 6 in. high, and have a really good root system, they may either be potted up into large pots or boxes or they may be planted out in the border.

Planting out in the border. The border should be dug over shallowly and compost of properly rotted vegetable refuse should be added at the rate of one good barrowload to 10 sq. yds. When compost is not available, damped sedge peat should be used. The alternative is to leave the soil raked level

and apply the powdery compost all over the soil 1 in. deep.
A light dressing of garden lime should be applied on the
surface at 4 oz to the square yard if shallow digging is done.

Before planting, care should be taken to see that the soil is
at a temperature of not less than 58°F. When plants are put
in soil of a lower temperature, the roots die, and though the

Ready for planting – first truss of flowers showing

plant may recover the cropping capacity is seriously lessened.
To ensure this, the house should be heated for at least a
fortnight before planting.

A hole should be made with a trowel large enough to
accommodate the plant and pot. The plants should stand in
their holes still in their pots for two or three days before being
knocked out, and by this time the roots of the plants will have
become acclimatized.

The plant may then be knocked out of the pot and dropped
into the hole, and pressed down firmly so that the top of the
ball is just below the level of the soil. Never put loose soil
around the collar of the plant because it is through this loose

soil that the wireworm can work and do damage. If the ball of
soil is exposed and hard, wireworms cannot get through.

The plant may best be removed from the pot by turning it
upside down and passing the stem between the second and
third fingers of the left hand. The rim of the pot should then
be tapped sharply on the bench or on a stone and the ball of
roots will be freed. The pot can then be taken off with the right
hand and put to one side when of course the actual operation
of putting the ball of soil in the hole provided can proceed.

Watering after planting. The plants should be watered for two or
three days after planting and again a week later. This should
be done with a can and a fine rose. After this, the plants in
the border should not be watered for a considerable time. In a
well-prepared border no water should be necessary until the
flowers of the second flower truss are opening in six or seven
weeks time. If water is given earlier, the plants are apt to
'run away' and they thus put all their energy into making
foliage growth rather than fruit.

In pots and boxes, watering may be necessary every two
days, it much depends on conditions. The ideal is only to
water the plant when it really needs it.

When a plant wants watering it has a distinctive appearance. It starts looking dull and grey, the leaves may start to
droop.

Ventilation. It should be possible to ventilate during the day,
and everything should be done to keep the air buoyant. The
temperature should not drop below 60°F for this reason.

Initial manuring. In addition to the properly composted vegetable refuse forked in at one good barrowload to 10 sq. yds or
applied as a top dressing, a complete organic fertilizer like
ground hoof and horn, or fish manure, should be given at
4 oz to the square yard.

Planting in pots or boxes. If tomatoes are to be grown in pots,
boxes or troughs, the soil-less compost should be placed in
position a week or so beforehand to warm. The plants intended
for this treatment should be grown on for three or four weeks
in their 3-in. pots and may then be potted on into 5-in. pots
for a similar period. After this they should be ready for trans-
ference into their final home, a 10-in. pot or of course a box
or trough. Plants may be put directly into their final pots with
equally good results as when given so many potting 'shifts'.

A heavy crop of tomatoes growing in pots on the left and in the soil of the greenhouse on the right

When transferring, it is important to disturb the root system as little as possible. Care should be taken to carry out the instructions given on potting on pages 41–2.

The pot, box or trough should never be filled higher than 4 in. from the top so as to allow for top dressings being added later. Planting should be done as advised for the border.

Water carefully in the early stages, or soft growth will result. It is better not to water till the first truss has set and to try and keep the plants going by syringings overhead until this period. Feed when the first two trusses have set with liquid Farmura, in accordance with instructions on the bottle. A weekly dose will usually be necessary. Stopping may be done at the third or fourth truss if there is no further room for the tops of the plants, or if they are to be used as a catchcrop.

Planting on Tom Bags. The Tom Bag contains Alexpeat Tomato Compost which is specially formulated to produce the right type of good firm close jointed growth, with broad dark green leaves and well-developed flower trusses. The Tomato Compost contains all the major, minor and trace elements, both in available and slow release forms, and in the correct balance with the emphasis on potash, to give the tomato plants a good start, and encourage the development of high quality sound firm fruit. Use four tomatoes per bag for short and medium term crops, three for long term crops.

Top dressings in the border or pot. The plants for the border may be given a top dressing every 14 days consisting of muriate or sulphate of potash at 1 oz to the square yard and dried blood at $\frac{1}{4}$ oz to the square yard. This mixture may be mixed together beforehand. Those who wish to buy an organic fertilizer like a fish manure should always be willing to add wood ashes, 3 parts bone meal and 5 parts dried blood.

When the plant has grown and the fifth truss has set, a more complicated dressing may be given, consisting of 3 parts of wood ashes, three parts bone meal and 5 parts dried blood. This may be applied at 3 oz to the square yard. (There are special organic fertilizers compounded for the purpose.) After this the plants should show considerable vigour and the normal top dressing may be resumed again. In the pot when two or three clusters of fruit have set, a top dressing of a soil-less compost may be given. This means applying 2 in. of soil. Six weeks afterwards another such top dressing may be necessary, and after each application a good watering should be given to settle the soil.

Pot plants always require more watering and manuring than plants in the border. When the plants are growing it is often necessary to water every day, and it is advisable to add to the water twice a week the Farmura.

Training. The rows of tomatoes in the house may either run across or lengthwise and whichever method is adopted wires should be stretched tightly along the ground from one end of the house to the other so that these can be used for anchoring the trellis or string up which the plants may be trained. It is quite easy then to make the holes with a dibber or planting tool ready to receive the tomatoes. When planting across the house it is usual to have double rows, i.e. two rows 18 in. apart with 15 in. between the plants and then a space of 27 in. between the next pair of rows. A main pathway should run down the centre of the house.

Fix a 12-gauge wire overhead and tie the 4-ply fillis or string from the top wire to the bottom wire and as the plant grows, twist it around the fillis. Another method is to put a bamboo or galvanized rod to each plant and tie the fillis to the short bamboo. It is a mistake to tie the string to the base of the plant as some gardeners do, for then there is always the danger when working among tomatoes of pulling the plants up.

Temperature. During growth the minimum night temperature should never fall below 63°F and never be above 75°F. In bright sunny weather a higher temperature can be allowed than in dull weather. In bright weather the plants make starch. Plants make plenty of starch and if the temperatures are not kept up it is difficult to 'move' them afterwards. The day temperatures in a tomato house should be from 63–65°F, but may rise from sun heat to 70°F or even 80°F.

Ventilation. It is always better to let the temperature of the house rise and keep the plants cool by overhead syringing, certainly in May or early June. From June onwards it is usually possible to leave on a little ventilation even at night-time and to increase this in hot weather. Cladosporium or mildew (mould) invariably appears if the heat is cut off in June and the houses closed down early in order to try and conserve sun heat. Always try and keep a little pipe-heat going plus ventilation, so as to ensure air movement. The doors at either end of the houses may be left open in the summer months, on calm days, but never when strong winds are blowing. Winds cause injury to plants and dry out the soil. End-on ventilation is always useful especially at the 'corners' of large houses.

Overhead damping. To ensure a good set, the atmosphere should contain a certain amount of moisture for the pollen to germinate. On bright sunny days syringing overhead may be done, but this is never advisable on a full day. There is never any need to tap a plant in order to shake the pollen as so many gardeners advise.

Side shoots and stopping. The side shoots must be removed. Allow the first six to stay on the plant till they are 6 in. long, as these assist in the development of the tomato in its early stages. Remove the side shoots by making them snap out. This can be done by giving them a sharp pull sideways. No stumps should ever be left to become infected with grey mould or this may encircle the stem and kill the plant. It is best to do the dis-shooting early in the morning.

It is always possible to train a side shoot up in place of the main stem if the latter gets damaged. Some gardeners prefer to grow their tomato plants on two stems and then of course they allow one of the lowest of the side shoots to grow naturally.

The practice of stopping is that of pinching off the growing point with the object of causing the lower trusses to mature earlier, and this is done say just above the fourth truss if very early fruit is wanted. As the total weight of crops is adversely affected it is not a practice to be encouraged. Stopping should therefore never be done till the plant has reached the top of the house, or at the latest about six weeks before pulling the plants out, whichever is the sooner.

Defoliation. The removal of leaves should always be done with great caution. The first operation is usually carried out when five trusses have set and then all the lower leaves between soil level and the first trusses are cut off. A fortnight later it is possible to remove the bottom half of the leaves between the second and fourth truss but only if the foliage is very dense. One of the simplest ways of removing these is to hold the stalk 2 in. from the main stem and then to give a sharp pull upwards.

Never carry out indiscriminate defoliation but always feel free to cut off any leaves that start to turn yellow.

Syringing and watering. It is a good plan to syringe the plants overhead on bright days as this helps to distribute the pollen and so assist fertilization. Once the plants have got to their maximum height further overhead syringing should not be carried out. It is then that the top shoots should be given a little more freedom so that shade to the flowers and fruits is provided.

If adequate flooding has been done in the winter it will not be necessary to water for six weeks after planting, apart of course from the original ball watering as the plant is put into position. It is as well to reduce watering to a minimum in April as this reduces the soil temperature, and as a result root troubles may develop. Water so that the end of the hose or can is kept close to the soil to prevent the lower fruits becoming splashed, for when this happens diseases may result. Water in the morning if possible. From June onwards water once a week, though on the very dry soils, twice a week. When watering put on plenty, and if the surface becomes hard it should be broken up with a fork to allow the water to pass through.

Top mulching. It helps to cover the surface of the soil with 6 in. of straw or damped sedge peat. This may be put on in May or early June. Peat is excellent because the plants may root into it.

*A Crittall greenhouse, 8ft. 4ins. ×
8ft. 7ins., with a louvre and roof
vent. Note the sliding door, and the
slanting sides which reduce the
amount of sunlight lost by reflection.
A small outside frame is also shown.*
CRITTALL WARMLIFE LTD.

*Only the wealthy amateur can look forward to a Clyde 22' wide, with double doors and
continuous ventilators, but it can be used for growing a wide variety of vegetables, including
potatoes, beans and cabbages, as well as decorative plants. ALITEX LTD.*

Standard metal-frame bench (various sizes, $2' \times 4'$, $2' \times 6'$, $3' \times 4'$, $3' \times 6'$). EDWARD OWEN LTD.

Standard roof ventilator, $4' \times 2'$. Extra ventilators are easily added to this house. EDWARD OWEN LTD.

Side of house showing adjustable louvre-type ventilators. EDWARD OWEN LTD.

Portsmouth 20/3. A view in a Garden Centre greenhouse showing slatted mats erected for shading. ALITEX LTD.

Shading. In very bright summers a certain amount of shading may be done to the roof in order to prevent sun scorch. The outside of the houses may be syringed over with a little lime-wash or some of the proprietary mixtures advertised for the purpose.

Varieties that do well in some districts often do poorly in others. Some varieties are specially suited to newly prepared land but are quite unsuited to land that has grown tomatoes for years.

Cucumbers

The cucumber is one of the oldest vegetables known. It has been popular in China and Egypt for thousands of years, and is now grown by the million in this country.

To grow cucumbers successfully a great deal of atmospheric moisture is required. This means that keeping the woodwork of the house in perfect condition is essential. It is always worthwhile painting the inside of the house every year, for not only does this preserve the wood, but kills resting disease spores and hiding insects. The wire supports, that run the length of the house, should be 6 in. apart. There should be a heating system installed which will always keep the house at a temperature of not less than 65°F at night time even in the coldest weather. It is equally important to ensure perfect

A heavy crop of 'Telegraph' cucumbers

drainage because a considerable amount of water has to be used every season, and it must be able to get away or root troubles will soon start.

Propagation. The actual time of sowing depends on when the planting has to be done. In winter two months are allowed from the time of sowing to planting, and in the summer and autumn six weeks are sufficient. Thus a sowing made in mid December allows for planting in the middle of February.

The seed should be sown in the John Innes seed compost or Alex Soil-less Compost (see page 40) the seeds being placed on their sides $\frac{1}{2}$ in. or so deep. The pots should be stood where there is plenty of bottom heat, a covering being made with glass and brown paper as for tomatoes. The temperature of the house at this stage should never be allowed to fall below 70°F at night-time.

Potting up. In ten days or a fortnight the plants may be potted up into 3-in. pots using the John Innes No. 2 or Alex Soil-less Compost. Cucumbers should not be potted firmly, soil should just be consolidated around the seedlings, but never pressed. Each plant should be inserted up to the seed leaf. A good watering should be given with water at the same temperature as the house, immediately afterwards. After this, watering need only be done when the soil appears dry, but this often means once a day! Good root development cannot take place in soil that is over-wet.

If the beds are not ready to receive the plants they should be potted on in 5-in. pots. This may be in a fortnight's time. The same compost may be used. The plants should be staked well before they start to flop over, and in five weeks time from this second potting they should be planted out.

A humid atmosphere should be kept in the greenhouse all the time.

Preparation of bed. A cucumber bed should be made of material that will keep open for as long as possible. This is important because of the large quantity of water that has to be thrown about in a cucumber house and which tends to compress the soil.

A normal bed is made up of equal parts of old straw and soil in alternate layers.

The bed should be made a fortnight before planting, first a layer of straw and then a layer of soil and so on, three layers of each in all. The bed should be about 2 ft wide, and should be well watered, so as to wet the straw thoroughly.

The bed should stand on well-drained soil, or on a concrete base over which a layer of garden lime has been placed 2–3 in. thick. This lime needs replacing every year.

Ventilation. Ventilation is rarely necessary, and air should be admitted with caution. In July the ventilators may be opened slightly on the leeward side to change the air in the house.

Temperature. The atmosphere of a cucumber house must never feel dry, and a brisk temperature must be maintained at all times. Damping down should be done night and morning, and syringing at mid-day. The night temperature should be about 70°F and in the daytime owing to sun-heat may rise to 90°F. When damping down, a gallon of water is often used to every three plants.

Training. The cucumber should be trained up wires, no side growth or lateral being left on the young plant below the first wire. The main stem should be allowed to go up to the roof of the house, the laterals being stopped when the second leaf has been produced. New sub-laterals are then produced and these are stopped after the second leaf and so on. Flowers may be produced on the main stem. Cucumbers should never be allowed to develop here. All male and female flowers on the main stem should therefore be removed, and all male flowers on the rest of the plant. The males cause the cucumber fruits to swell and be less palatable.

Apart from this, all dead leaves should be removed, as well as all young fruits showing disease. A gardener should aim at having two fruit-bearing joints on every lateral, and not more than three breaks.

Top dressings. These should be given three weeks after planting, and should consist in the first place of straw or strawy stable manure. A week later a top dressing of soil may be given all over the bed. The soil should be wheeled into the house twelve hours before it is required for use. Cucumber fruits usually come in flushes, and it is necessary to top dress after each flush.

Withholding water. As much harm is done to cucumbers by over-watering as under-watering. It is usually only necessary to soak the beds twice a week. If it is noticed that the young fruits that are coming on tend to damp off, water should be withheld for a week.

Shading. Shade should be given in very hot weather. Flour paste is best (then it can be used again) as the rays of light are not reflected back into the air as with lime wash. One 5-in. potful of ordinary flour will give 3 gallons of shading.

Lettuce

Lettuces may be grown under glass in a cool house at almost any period of the year. Naturally they are usually grown during the months when it is difficult to obtain them outside. There are two main crops, the autumn and spring.

Lettuces are a good catch crop to follow tomatoes, and may be used as an inter-crop provided they are planted out before the tomatoes, as advised later.

A first planting is usually done between mid-September and mid-October so as to obtain well-hearted specimens during December and January, while a second planting is often carried out in December and January for the purpose of cutting during February and March. It is always better to have a whole house of lettuce rather than to try and use them for inter-planting tomatoes.

THE AUTUMN CROP

The seed should be sown on or about 15 September. Seed trays or shallow pans should be filled with the John Innes seed Compost or Alexpeat compost to within $\frac{1}{4}$ in. of the top; after watering thoroughly the seed should be sown. With the standard seed box 200 seeds are necessary, evenly spaced.

A small quantity of the same compost should be sifted over the seeds, and the boxes may then be covered with a sheet of glass and dark paper. Germination should take place in four days, and the glass and paper should then be removed.

During this time the boxes should be on the benches of a house kept at the temperature of about 60–65°F. In eight days' time the baby seedlings should be pricked out into further seed trays (usual size) 54 seedlings per tray. The John Innes or Alex potting compost should now be used. The trays should remain on the bench in the glasshouse at a temperature of from 55–60°F.

PREPARATION OF BORDER AND PLANTING

In the glasshouses where the lettuces are to be planted out, the soil should have been prepared ready for the tomato crop in the spring. The lettuce planting should take place the first week in October, the soil being on the compact side. The top $\frac{1}{2}$ in. of soil should be raked as fine as possible, all the surface stones should be removed, for these cool down more quickly at night than the soil round about.

After planting, the seedlings should be watered with water at the same temperature as the house, and through a fine rose. Care should be taken not to wet the leaves, so always hold the rose of the can low down in between the rows of plants.

Further watering may be done as required, and hoeing should be carried out regularly. If water is not given regularly, the lettuce plants wilt, and then the lower leaves touch the ground and are attacked by botrytis. If water is regularly given the leaves stand up. Again it may be emphasized that the leaves of the plant should not be wetted, but only the soil.

Decaying leaves. All decaying leaves, drying leaves and so on should be removed directly they are seen, with a sharp knife. These may be infected with a serious form of botrytis. The leaves should be burnt immediately.

Temperatures. When the lettuces are growing, the temperature should not exceed 55°F at night-time. In certain cases, if it is thought the crop is growing too slowly, the temperature may be increased to 60°F for a fortnight, and then drop down to 55°F once more or perhaps even to 50°F.

Never attempt to force the crop. Always give ventilation on all favourable occasions. Have a little pipe-heat if you can and keep the ventilators open a little to maintain a buoyant atmosphere.

Hoeing. Hoe the soil between the plants two or three times in order to keep down weeds. Be very careful not to damage the plants when doing this work.

The spring crop. The spring crop should be treated in exactly the same way as the autumn crop, the seed being sown about 15 October. The seedlings should be pricked out as previously advised and the house may be planted up about 10 December.

Where an early crop of tomatoes is to follow, the lettuce should be planted 9 in. apart, and in such a way that the tomato plants may be put out in between them, as they are growing, when the time comes.

French beans

After the middle of September French beans have to be grown
in pots in the greenhouse; 10-in. pots are usually most convenient, and these after being well crocked should be filled
with the No. 2 John Innes Compost or the Alexpeat Compost.

The pots should be filled three quarters full and eight beans
should be placed around the edge of each pot $1\frac{1}{2}$ in. deep.
If all the beans grow, the number of plants should be reduced
to five. It is most important not to water the soil after seed
sowing. The beans germinate much better and do not 'damp
off' if the compost is kept on the dry side.

As the plants progress more of a similar compost may be
added until the soil reaches within 1 in. of the top of the pot.

General management. The plants should be syringed twice a day
to ensure that the flowers set properly and to keep down
red spiders. When the first pods are formed a watering may

Stake out as soon as plants develop

be given with a liquid manure. This may be obtained from any
horticultural sundriesman. Further feeds may be given once a
week after this.

Some sticks may be pushed into the soil to support the plants
as soon as they develop. The house should be ventilated
whenever possible so as to ensure robust growth. Care should
be taken not to allow draughts so that the plants do not get
chilled.

Temperatures. The temperature of the house should be from
55–60°F at night-time during the whole life of the plants, but
may be allowed to rise a few degrees during the day.

CLIMBING FRENCH BEANS

Climbing French beans are an alternative to the Bush French beans and may be grown in the same way as suggested for them. The seed is usually sown in the narrow border where the plants are to grow, and the vines are trained on wires or strings close to the light. They may also be grown up string or wires right the way through the house.

Whichever way the plants are supported they should be thinned out so that they grow 9–12 in. apart each way.

The earliest sowing, 8 per 3-in. pot, is usually done during mid-January especially in the south. In the north it is necessary to delay until the beginning of February, in some instances. Quicker results are achieved if the plants are raised in 3-in. pots and sown as advised for ordinary French beans. Planting is then done as for tomatoes (see page 60) to avoid a check in root development. In this case a light watering is given after planting to settle the soil around the ball of roots. Provide a string up which the plant is to grow and loop the top of the shoot to the string, tying it into position with raffia or green cotton 'twist'.

Damp the plants twice a day as the season advances and give two feeds with a liquid manure during the growing season. Be careful never to over-water or the roots will die off. Keep the plants free from red spider by syringing over regularly. Climbing French beans should always be pulled out of the house by late June and then a crop of late tomatoes may follow.

Radishes

Radishes may be sown on special beds made on the staging or directly in the border of the greenhouse. They do best in a low house because they are then not drawn so much. The border should be well worked, and should be rich in humus as the result of previous dressings of manure. The seed should be sown thinly, and not be covered with more than $\frac{1}{2}$-in. of soil made firm on the surface after sowing.

Seed sowing may be done any time between the middle of October and the middle of February. Radishes like plenty of water, and the greenhouse should be ventilated freely day and night once the plants have started to grow.

It is possible to take two crops of radishes in a greenhouse between the months of October and March. It is most important not to force, and the three essentials are light, air and moisture.

Marrows

It is possible to grow a trailing variety of marrow as a catch-crop, the idea being to train the stems up the purling posts in the houses. The plants are usually raised by sowing seeds singly in 3-in. pots and placing them on the staging of the house in the usual way. The plants are then set out as soon as possible at the base of the purlin posts where a special bed may have been prepared as for marrows in the open. When the flowers open, hand pollination is necessary to set the fruit and to do this the male flower is detached and the petals removed. The stamen is then rubbed over the stigma of the fruit producing flower.

As the flowers develop they are given some support by looping some fillis or raffia round the stalk of the fruit and tying it to the purlin posts. Side shoots that do not develop a marrow are completely removed.

Cut the fruits when they are 12 in. long. You will usually get four good marrows per plant. Don't forget to water regularly directly the plants start to crop for marrows are 90 per cent moisture.

Mustard and Cress

May be sown in boxes on soil placed on the staging or even directly in the beds. An attempt should be made to grow it and clear it in fourteen days.

The best results are obtained when the soil is sterilized or the John Innes Seed Compost or Alex Soil-less Compost may be used. This should be made fairly firm and should be well watered.

When the bulk of the moisture has drained away the seed should be sown rather thinly and should *not* be covered with soil. The boxes may be kept in the dark for a few days or can be covered with brown paper.

The cress takes four days longer than the mustard and so should be sown four days beforehand. If there is sufficient heat the mustard seed should germinate within three days. After this it should be ready to cut in a week.

Cauliflowers

Cauliflowers can be grown in the greenhouse in order to get a particularly early crop.

About 15 September the seed is sown on a prepared seed bed out of doors and covered with Access frames or cloches. When three rough leaves have developed, the seedlings are potted into 3-in. pots using a John Innes No. 2 Compost or Alex Soil-less Compost. The plants are then kept in a cold frame or cold glasshouse. Meanwhile the soil in the greenhouse is prepared as for tomatoes (see page 58) and the plants are put out about the third week of January in rows 2 ft apart, allowing 18 in. apart. Ball watering is done and from then onwards the temperature of the house must not fall below 48°F at night-time and must never go above 60°F by day. Water once a week, and be prepared to be liberal with ventilation if the weather gets warm. Syringe overhead on bright mornings.

RAISING VARIOUS VEGETABLES FOR PLANTING OUT

The greenhouse can be used to raise large numbers of plants for planting out of doors later. This is not quite the book to give details of this, and those who are interested should read my *Basic Book of Vegetable Growing* in this series.

Onions, celery and leeks are sown in January and February, New Zealand spinach, aubergines and maize are sown in March, outside tomatoes and ridge cucumbers can be brought on ready for planting out in June. Peas, French beans and runner beans may be raised in boxes or pots and be planted out directly the weather is warm enough.

9 Fruits under glass

The glasshouse can be used for growing many kinds of fruit. Almost every known fruit has been grown in this country under such conditions. Many, like pineapples for instance, need special pits and heat, but large numbers like grapes, peaches and nectarines may be grown in any ordinary house given the proper care and attention.

Vines

The year 1950 saw a great return to grape growing under glass. The horticultural press devoted much more space to the culture of this fruit, and specialist firms started advertising.

A stronger wiring system is needed for vine rods than for tomatoes or cucumbers. High temperatures are not required except in the case of Muscats, when flowering. As birds may give trouble when the berries ripen the openings of the ventilators are usually covered with small meshed wire netting.

The border. It is always easier – on the whole – for an amateur to grow a vine in a border outside. Efficient drainage is absolutely essential, and when preparing the border, the gardener has to see that the soil will remain fertile for eight or nine years. The roots of a vine should always be attracted to the surface and not into the subsoil.

Preparation of border. The soil should be taken out to a depth of $2\frac{1}{2}$ ft the bottom of the hole being then filled in with a 6-in. thickness of broken brickbats or stones. This drainage material should be covered with a 2-in. thickness of damped sedge peat and should be covered with a generous sprinkling of crushed bone. The remaining 2 ft may be filled in with a compost consisting of 6 parts good soil, 3 parts of good compost, $\frac{1}{2}$ part wood ashes, $\frac{1}{8}$ part of bonemeal and $\frac{1}{8}$ part of ground chalk. The ingredients should be mixed well together before being used. The hole should be filled in evenly and trodden down firmly.

Propagation. It is possible to propagate vines by means of

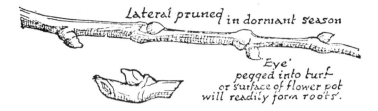

'Eye' pegged into turf and surface of flower pot will readily form roots

cuttings taken from well-ripened one-year old laterals. These cuttings should be of a length to contain about four buds. They should be struck in sandy soil in a greenhouse at a temperature of about 65°F. It is possible just to take one bud or eye off a lateral and plant it in the centre of a pot of soil in January or February so that the eye is exposed and the piece of wood at the base just buried. When the cuttings or eyes are well rooted they are usually potted on to 6- or 8-in. pots and it is in these latter that they will finish their first year's growth.

They are well ripened off in the late autumn and remain in a cold house until the beginning of the second year. They are then cut back to within two buds of their base. When growth starts, water should be given and the night temperature should be kept at about 55°F. At the end of the second year it is usually advisable to pot into 12-in. pots or to set the vines out in their permanent position.

Planting. Two- or three-year-old canes may be purchased, and if they are to be restricted to a single rod they may be put in as close as 3 ft apart. Where a rod is eventually going to be allowed to grow naturally it may need up to 20 ft of room.

Planting may take place in the autumn or in late March or early April. In the former case the vine should be planted without disturbing the roots, and in the latter case the soil should be shaken out so that they can be spread out carefully.

General cultivation – first year. The soil of the bed should be kept moist but not too wet, and a humid atmosphere should be obtained in the house. Ample ventilation must be provided especially during hot dry weather, or weak growth will result. First thing in the morning and first thing at night, the vine should be syringed over. It may be necessary to damp the house down during the day as well, should the weather be warm.

The first year's growth should be about 8 ft and this should be stopped towards the end of August. As the foliage shows signs of ripening water should be withheld. In December the rods should be cut back to within 6 ft of the ground exactly above a good strong bud.

Second year. The rods should be untied in February and allow to bend over so as to ensure that the buds break evenly. When growth has commenced it should be tied back to the wire again. The border should be given a good watering in March.

Two or three growths should now be seen at each eye. The smaller ones should be rubbed out, and the main one left to grow on. Fruit sometimes shows on these, but should be rubbed out.

When these breaks grow to about 1 ft in length they should be stopped, and the side growths which form afterwards should be cut to two joints. The end growth or leader should be allowed to grow naturally.

Third year. This should be the first fruiting year.

All the side growths should be cut back to one well-developed eye, and the leader reduced by about half. The rod should be allowed to bend over as before, and the weaker growths rubbed out after the rod is tied back again. (See second year.)

Every lateral should be showing fruit this year, but only eight bunches in all should be allowed. Heavier cropping than this ruins the constitution of the young rod.

Subsequent years. Each year the vine should be pruned in the winter by cutting back the laterals to one good plump bud, and the leader by half or a quarter as desired. After this, the rod should be painted over with a 5 per cent solution of a good tar distillate wash.

As the side growths develop in the spring, they should be stopped at two joints beyond the bunch of fruit or at one joint if there isn't space for a greater extension. The tendrils should be pinched off at the same time. The secondary shoots which grow out as a result of such a stopping should be pinched immediately beyond the first leaf and so on again and again throughout the season as they continue to grow.

The leading shoot of the vine is exempted from being

stopped when the rod is young, but is often pinched when the rod has grown to the top of the house.

Temperature. The temperature of the house when the vine starts to grow should be between 50 and 60°F. The temperature should rise gradually until it reaches a temperature of 70°F by the time the vine is in flower. When the grapes are set the temperature may again be lowered to 60°F until after the stoning period is passed. Then the temperature may rise again to 70°F.

When the grapes begin to colour the temperature should again be dropped to 65°F and in cold weather it is always better to have a slightly lower temperature than to maintain a high one with over-heated pipes.

Ventilation. Ventilation not only helps to control the temperature, but admits fresh air. Vines require little ventilation in the morning, but this may be increased as the day advances, the house being closed by stages in the afternoon, until the ventilators are shut right down in order to trap some of the sun heat. Vines need air when the grapes are starting to colour, and it is only then that the ventilator should be opened day and night.

Watering. It is most important to flood the vine border thoroughly each winter. It is surprising how much water the border will take, and in order to ensure that the subsoil is well wetted, it may be necessary to give 200 gallons. During the growing season the plants must have a sufficient supply of water also, a good flooding being given before flowering and another after thinning. In fact, the border should be kept well watered until the grapes start to colour and ripen.

Feeding. Once the berries are thinned, feeding should be liberal and Marinure or Farmura may be given once a fortnight when any watering is done.

Every winter after removing any loose strips of bark from off the rods and painting with a tar distillate wash, a liberal mulching of composted vegetable waste should be placed over the borders.

Winter work. The vinery should be cleared of all fallen leaves and the leaders shortened back. When young this will mean

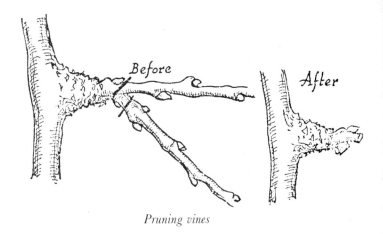

Pruning vines

leaving about 4 ft of growth and when the rod has reached the
top of its allotted span it will need cutting back almost entirely.
When the loose bark has been pulled off the rods and the tar
distillate wash applied to them all the prunings and other
debris may be removed before the mulching of dung or
vegetable refuse is put on as advised above.

Pollination. It is usually advisable to tap the rods in the middle
of the day, when the plants are in flower, in order to distribute
the pollen. In the case of Muscats the temperature will have
to be raised and this usually means closing the ventilators for
a few hours in the middle of the day. The atmosphere must
always be kept charged with moisture during this time, but
when fertilization has been completed the temperature may be
reduced.

Moisture. The rods will need spraying regularly with clean
water at the same temperature as the house in the early stages
to cause the buds to break freely, and in the later stages to
keep down red spider. Syringing should be discontinued as
the vines come into flower, and again later as the grapes start
to colour. Open the vents early to dry off the moisture on the
berries before the sun gets on them.

It is important to syringe regularly after the grapes have
been cut.

Thinning. Three times as many berries are produced on a
bunch as can ever come to perfection. If they are all left to
develop the berries get jammed, the inner ones may rot, and
the bunch will be spoiled.

Thinning should be done with care for the berries should never be handled nor should they touch human hair. A little forked stick should be made to hold the berries out, and the actual thinning should be done with a narrow pair of long pointed scissors.

Two thinnings are necessary, the first when the grapes are the size of sweet pea seed, and the second when they are the size of marrowfat peas. The inner berries should be cut out first, then the small berries, then the side berries. In the case of the larger bunches the shoulders should be tied up with raffia.

Stoning. The stoning period usually lasts two or three weeks. If too much water is given at this time the skin of the berries may crack. The house needs ventilating but draughts must be avoided, and the rods should be syringed.

Peaches and Nectarines

As the nectarine is a smooth skinned type of peach these two are dealt with under one heading.

Fan-shaped trees with a short stem are usually grown on wires 1 ft or 18 in. away from the glass of the house, or against the back wall.

The border. The soil should be dug out to a depth of $2\frac{1}{2}$ ft the hole being 5 ft long and 3 ft wide. In the bottom of the hole put in a 4-in. layer of coarse rubble or stones, and above these a layer of coarse sedge peat 2 in. deep should be placed. The hole should then be filled in with the following compost: 6 parts good soil, 1 part ground chalk, $\frac{1}{8}$ part bone-meal and $\frac{1}{8}$ part wood ashes.

Planting. This should be done in the autumn, say October or November, care being taken to see that there is at least 5 in. between the trunk of the tree and the brickwork. The roots should be spread out evenly and shallowly, and the soil should be trodden in firmly around it. Care should be taken never to bury the union of the stock and scion where the grafting and budding has taken place.

First year. The great thing in the first year is to get the tree firmly established. In January damped sedge peat should be applied all over the ground to a depth of 2 in. for 3 ft around the stem of the tree. Pruning is done at the same time by shortening the shoots to half their length.

Manuring. Dried blood may be applied at 2 oz to the square yard early in February. In November or December a good fish manure should be given at the rate of 3 oz per square yard. After the fruit has stoned a liquid feed may be given like Farmura.

Each year garden lime may be applied after the fruit is picked at the rate of 4 oz to the square yard. This will not be necessary if the ground is naturally chalky.

Watering. Plenty of water should be applied in the spring and summer months whenever the soil gets dry. A good flooding is necessary in the winter too. The branches and leaves of the tree should be syringed after the fruit has set until the time when it begins to ripen. Syringing should continue after harvesting.

Pruning. Both the peach and the nectarine flower on the last year's well-ripened growths, and on a few short spurs. The

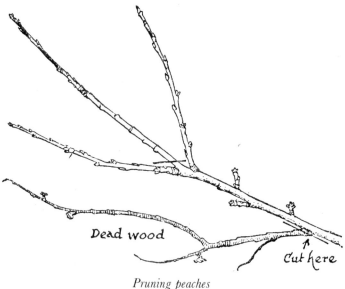

Pruning peaches

pruner's main object is to try and furnish the tree with equal sized branches radiating evenly from the main stem.

The aim should be to produce the tree's lower branches first of all and then to allow the centre of the fan to be filled in afterwards.

The peach should be trained on wires which are securely

fastened 4 in. away from the wall. It is on to these wires spaced 12 or 18 in. apart that the growth should be tied after the trees have been pruned. In the winter the older growths are removed and the younger not over-strong shoots retained. The pruner should aim at a tree which has well-ripened young growths spaced 4 in. apart all over.

Much pruning has to be done in the summer for from each young shoot retained in the winter large numbers of laterals grow out in the spring. Only three, or at the most, four of these should be kept, and the surplus should be rubbed out with the thumb and forefinger when they are $\frac{1}{2}$ in. long. A growth should be left at the base of each length of fruiting wood so that this may take the place of this wood when the fruit has been picked. The operation of dis-shooting should be extended over a period of ten days.

A tree that crops heavily makes less wood than a tree that doesn't fruit. Trees tending to make too much growth should be root-pruned.

Sometimes a shoot is left near a fruit for the purpose 'of drawing the sap'. This should be stopped at six leaves.

Pollination. All varieties of peaches and nectarines are self-fertile, but it is best to help pollination by means of a rabbit's tail attached to a short length of bamboo. This is used to titillate the flowers.

Temperatures. The house should be kept at a temperature of about 50°F when the trees are in flower. After this the temperature should be increased to 55 or 60°F at night-time – gradually. During the daytime the temperature may rise to 75°F.

Mulching. After flowering it is advisable to mulch with damped sedge peat as suggested under the heading First Year (see page 79).

Thinning. After the fruits have stoned properly the fruit should be thinned so as to only leave 1 per sq. ft in the case of peaches and 1 per 9 sq. in. in the case of nectarines. This thinning is usually done in two periods.

General management. Surplus shoots are removed during the summer but growths required may be kept tied in.

Towards the end of the summer, full air should be admitted night and day, so as to ensure the proper ripening of the fruit. Towards October water should be withheld gradually.

Nets should be placed in position to catch the falling fruit, the ripest being removed daily. When all the fruit has been gathered the house should be given a thorough syringing.

The Fig

The fig is interesting in that the flowers are borne in a pear-shaped inflorescence. The so-called fruit is really a cavernous fruit stalk with an opening at the top. In this hollow receptacle the two kinds of flowers are borne, male and female.

Under glass, figs may be grown as bush trees in pots, or in the border, but are more often grown as fan-trained trees against the back wall, or on a wire trellis in the house.

Preparation. The soil should be taken out 2 ft deep and a 4 in. layer of stony rubble placed in the bottom. This should be rammed down and is there to act as drainage and to help prevent the roots coming through into unpleasant subsoil.

The hole should then be filled in with good soil to a barrow-load of which has been added two large handfuls of bonemeal, two handfuls of wood ashes and a handful of ground chalk. This soil mixture should be made firm.

A border $3\frac{1}{2}$ ft wide and $1\frac{1}{2}$ ft deep should be quite good enough for a fig. A restricted root run seems to produce the right kind of short jointed shoot which crops heavily.

Starting into growth. In a house devoted to the fig only, it is usual to start the trees into growth about January. The night temperature should then be 60°F and during fine days may rise to 80°F midday with sun-heat.

The house should be syringed twice daily, in the morning and in the afternoon.

Stopping. When the side shoots have made four leaves, the growing point should be pinched out and all sub-laterals should also be pinched at four leaves.

The baby fruit which has set on last year's wood should soon start to swell and it is then that plenty of water should be applied. Twice a week feed with liquid manure in the water used for watering.

This first crop should ripen in June.

Second crop. A second crop should be produced on the young wood which has probably been stopped when 8 in. long and should be ready to pick in August. A moist atmosphere should be kept up in the house by frequent syringing and the temperature may now rise to 90°F during the day with the sun. It may be necessary to shut up the house early in the afternoon to bottle up the sun-heat.

The most successful fig growers are those who keep the glass of the greenhouse perfectly clean, for an abundance of light is essential.

The three-crop system. Some growers like to take three crops a year and so they start the fig into growth in December, keeping the house at a temperature of 80°F. Picking should then commence at the end of March. The second crop is borne on the current year's growth which ripens in May and June. The third crop, usually small fruit, ripens in July.

It is important to try and restrict the root run of the fig or otherwise excessive growth results at the expense of fruiting. Never let the roots, for instance, run *outside* the house.

When the fruits start to swell feed with Farmura or Maxi-crop at intervals of four days, giving a good dose on each occasion.

Very little ventilation is necessary until ripening time, but when the fruits start to colour air must be given. No syringing or damping down should be done directly ripening starts.

Pruning. The fig is most amenable to pruning and may be pruned as desired in the winter. The shoots should be thinned where necessary and the dead wood removed. A pruner should bear in mind that the first crop is produced on short-jointed, well-ripened wood of the preceding year's growth.

The Melon

The melon should be grown in similar manner to the cucumber (see Chapter 8) and is quite a suitable crop for the low span roof greenhouse.

Propagation. The seed is usually sown the first week in January, although later sowings are possible; 3-in. pots are chosen for this purpose, and after being cleaned and crocked are filled with the John Innes Seed Compost or Alex Soil-less Compost. Two seeds are then sown per pot by pushing them in $\frac{1}{4}$ in. deep. If both germinate, the stronger plant of the two should be selected. It is advisable to warm the pots and the soil before sowing the seed.

The pots should then be stood over the pipes in a greenhouse or plunged in a hotbed up to the rim. They should be covered with glass and a sheet of brown paper and the temperature in the greenhouse should then be at 75–80°F.

A good crop of Dutch net melons, many of them supported by nets

Directly the seedlings appear, the glass and paper should be removed and the young plant may then be stood on a shelf near the glass of the house.

Potting on. When the plants are 3 or 4 in. high and are well rooted they may be potted on into 5-in. pots, the John Innes Potting Compost or Alex Soil-less Compost being used (see page 41).

Throughout the growth of the plant regular syringings should be done with water at the same temperature as the house, in order to keep the atmosphere moist.

Making the beds. In the greenhouse, the beds in which the melons are to grow should be made up some days before they are required so that the soil can warm up. It is usual to place in position a layer of turves, grass side downwards; on the turves a ridge 1 ft high and 8 in. wide of special compost is then placed, this ridge being made moderately firm. A similar compost as advised for the potting is suitable. The plants should be put in quite firmly 18 in. apart, and a little stake put in next to them to keep them upright. It may be necessary to tie this stake to the first wire.

Some gardeners believe in putting a metal collar around each plant about the size of an ordinary circular tobacco tin. Instructions are then given that no one must water inside the collar, for what is known as collar-rot may take place if this is done.

Set the ball of soil in the bed so that half of it is above the soil level. Then as watering proceeds the soil of the ball will gradually fall away and the top of the roots is exposed. This does prevent collar-rot. When pots are cheap, the bottom of the pot can be knocked off and the plant then set in the soil, pot and all. The roots grow into the compost and no watering is done inside the pot.

Training. The plant should be allowed to run up to the second wire and should then be stopped to allow the side shoots to develop. Any that grow out below the first wire should be pinched back.

When the flowers have set, and the fruits are starting to swell, not more than two, or at the most, three melons should be allowed per plant. The surplus fruits should be removed a few at a time, making certain to keep those which are approximately the same size.

Three or four laterals are usually taken on either side of the stem but further growth is restricted so as to prevent overcrowding.

Pollination. When five or six female blooms are fully expanded, pollen may be transferred from the male flowers by means of a rabbit's tail to the females. Bees may be allowed to work in a melon house, but, incidentally, *never* in a cucumber house. During the middle of the day when it is sunny a free circulation of air should be encouraged to help dry the foliage. This helps in pollination.

Temperature and watering. Tepid water should always be used. The collar should be kept dry, but apart from this the soil around the roots should be kept on the moist side.

Syringing may be done twice daily, and draughts should be avoided. On the whole, melons are kept dryer than cucumbers.

A little extra water may be given as the melons come into flower, but this should be discontinued as the flowers open. At this time syringing should only be done once – in the afternoon. When the fruit shows signs of changing colour withhold all moisture, and give free ventilation.

From planting date until the ripening of the fruits the temperature of the house should be 70°F.

Manuring. As the roots appear through the compost, top dressings may be given of good soil mixed equally with well-decayed old composted vegetable waste. This compost should be left in the house for a day to get warm.

When the fruits are swelling, Farmura may be given at the rate of say 2 gallons of feed per three plants once a week.

Some gardeners prefer to give dried blood twice at intervals of 14 days from the time the fruits are the size of cricket balls.

General remarks. The fruit as it ripens should always be supported by nets. It is about then that the humidity and temperature may be reduced and water to the roots also.

January sowings ensure a good crop from the first week of May onwards, and June sowings from the end of August onwards.

Strawberries

Strawberries out of season are always attractive, though they perhaps have not quite the flavour of those grown outside.

Propagation. The runners required should be from healthy vigorous parents from a good strain. Royal Sovereign is probably the only variety that is worth forcing, but the strain Malling 47 is the best, when you can get it.

The parents should be set out in August or September and are thus established before the winter sets in. In late March they are given a dressing of meat and bonemeal at 3 oz to the square yard, and sulphate of potash at 1 oz to the square yard. When the blossom trusses develop they are removed and soon after this the runners should begin to appear.

Three-inch pots should then be soaked in water for two or three hours and after crocking should be filled with the John Innes Potting Compost or Alex Soil-less Compost. The soil should be firm, sufficient space being left to allow for watering. A drill should then be drawn V-shaped and 3 to 4 in. deep down one side of each row of the parent plants. A continuous row of pots should then be placed in the prepared drill. The drill should then be filled in so that the pots are level when plunged.

As the runners develop one should be pegged into the top of each pot with wire pegs like hairpins.

When the runners are well rooted they should be severed from their parents, and a week later they may be potted on into 5-in. pots using a similar compost. The 3-in. pots should be watered thoroughly before potting and if earthworms are suspected a $\frac{1}{4}$ oz of corrosive sublimate should be dissolved in

3 gallons of water to kill them. Care should be taken for this chemical is a deadly poison, and as its name suggests is corrosive to metal containers.

Each plant should be so potted that the crown points to the *edge*, and so that the plant itself is towards the edge. Firm potting is essential. For a week these pots should remain in the shade and afterwards may be stood on a good ash base in full sun.

Summer work. The pots on the ash beds should be syringed night and morning and Farmura in solution may be given twice a week at first and later every time the plants are watered, $\frac{1}{4}$ oz is sufficient for a $2\frac{1}{2}$ gallon can of water. The pots should be arranged so that all the crowns point south and stood sufficiently far apart to ensure that the foliage doesn't overlap.

Autumn work. During the third week of October, the pots should be laid on their sides and a fortnight later the plants should be placed in a cold frame plunged in peat moss. If this is not available the pots should be stacked on their sides in tiers against the wall, ashes being used to keep the pots level. The crowns should point outwards from the wall.

Winter work. Early in January the plants may be taken into the greenhouse at a temperature of 40–45°F at night and 50°F during the day. Strawberries must be forced slowly until they are well into flower. Three weeks later the plants should be dipped in a 3 per cent solution of lime-sulphur, and afterwards $\frac{1}{4}$-in. of top soil should be scraped off each pot, and this should be replaced with some warm John Innes Potting Compost or Alex Soil-less Compost.

The plants should be syringed once a day for the first fortnight and twice a day afterwards.

When the plants come into flower the temperature should be raised to 55°F at night and 65°F in the day. Hand pollination should be done with a rabbit's tail.

The fruits as they swell should be thinned, not more than 10 to 15 berries being left per pot. Each fruiting truss should hang over the edge of the pot, and this is the advantage of potting the crown well to the side.

Forcing. When the fruits start to swell the temperature may be raised to 65°F at night-time and 70°F or even more during the day. It is still necessary to syringe the plants twice a day until the berries start to colour, when such spraying should be discontinued. When the fruits start to colour a little liquid manure may be given. A seaweed liquid manure is ideal for this purpose. The pots will need watering almost daily in addition.

General remarks. It is possible to force strawberries by bringing them into heat before Christmas, but really heavy crops are never produced if this is done.

Pot fruits

It is possible to grow apples, cherries, pears and plums in pots under glass, indeed, vines, figs, peaches, nectarines and apricots may be grown in this way also.

Trees in pots are portable and can be moved whenever necessary. The pot should be stood on bricks so as to leave the drainage openings clear and the trees are then completely under control. A great variety of fruits may be grown successfully in one house, the trees being taken outside once the fruit has been gathered.

The early varieties of apricots, nectarines and peaches are often carried outside to make room for plums, and later kinds. Thus a succession is provided for.

Rotation. A convenient rotation for a fruit house is pot fruits followed by pot chrysanthemums. The advantage of these two crops is that they neither of them need a great deal of heat. A 4-in. hot water pipe therefore in the front and the back of a lean-to will suffice, but the little warmth provided assists in the setting of the fruit and the swelling of the crop and should be sufficient to exclude the frost at night-time in the case of the chrysanthemums.

Potting. Pots ranging from 10 in. to 18 in. are usually used, the compost consisting of two thirds soil and one third well-decayed manure; a little broken brick may be added for the stone fruits. The plants will not need annual repotting, and it should only be necessary to remove some of the loose surface soil and replace with the John Innes Potting Compost or Alex Soil-less Compost.

When trees require a shift they should be knocked out of the pots, the ball should be loosened, the longest roots shortened and the tree potted on into a pot one size larger. At each potting, sufficient space should be left below the rim for watering.

Temperatures and ventilation. The pots may be stood outside during the winter, and be brought in early in March, or they may, of course, stay in the house all the year. Once inside, the temperature should be between 40–45°F at night-time, directly the blossoms are visible. From the fruit setting to the early part of June 50°F should be aimed at, and from June onwards the ventilators should remain open day and night until October or until the pots are stood outside to make room for the chrysanthemums.

Syringing. The pots should be syringed from the time the fruits set until they commence to ripen. The water used should be the same temperature as the house and should be applied vigorously. This is best done as the sun declines, but sufficiently early so that the foliage is fairly dry before nightfall.

Pruning and spraying. There is not the room to deal with pruning and spraying in detail in a book of this character, but full instructions will be found in a companion volume, the *Basic Book of Fruit Growing* in this series.

10 Flowers under glass.
Annuals and biennials

The warmth and protection of a glasshouse opens up far greater possibilities for the flower grower who possesses one than for the less fortunate grower who does not. In this chapter we start with the annuals, the easiest subjects but some of the most colourful and welcome, when grown out of season.

Subsequent chapters tell of bulb forcing, foliage plants and a host of lovely perennial pot plants – all possible to be grown to perfection by the keen glasshouse owner.

Annuals for the greenhouse decoration may be divided into two classes. There are the tender annuals which will be discussed in the second part of this chapter; and also many hardy and half-hardy annuals which succeed in pots and which may be forced in spring to flower from February till May. Spring sowings will also produce plants to flower in late summer or autumn.

SEED SOWING

For spring flowering the seeds should be sown late in August or early in September, and for summer and autumn flowering one sowing should be made in March, and another at the end of April.

Probably the best plan is to sow the seeds straight into small pots, but they may be sown in boxes (with the exception of mignonette, which dislikes disturbance) and pricked off singly into pots when large enough. Pots, 2 or 3 in. in diameter, should be crocked and half-filled with the John Innes No. 1 Seed Compost or Alex Soil-less Compost, which should be made fairly firm and watered well with a fine rose. When the surplus moisture has drained away, two or three seeds should be sown in the centre of each pot and lightly covered with some finely sifted compost. The pots should then be placed in a cold frame or cool house and covered with sheets of glass and brown paper until germination has taken place.

As soon as the seedlings show above the soil, the paper and

glass should be removed, and the pots gradually introduced into strong light, when they should be placed on shelves in a cool house near to the glass, or the autumn-sown ones may remain in a cold frame until October. When large enough they should be thinned down to one per pot, retaining the strongest and most healthy-looking in each case.

It is important that annuals should not be starved in their early stages. As they grow, they should be top-dressed gradually until the pots are filled with compost to within about $\frac{1}{2}$ in. of their tops. When the pots are comfortably filled with roots they should be potted on into their flowering pots, 5 or 6 in. in diameter. The compost used this time should be the John Innes Potting Compost No. 2, or Alex Soil-less Compost No. 2.

PINCHING

The seedlings should be pinched back two or three times to promote bushy growth, except in the case of stocks, salpiglossis, mignonette and scabious which branch more or less naturally.

GENERAL CULTURE

Autumn-sown annuals. During the winter the roots should be kept only just moist, and the atmosphere as dry as possible, otherwise the seedlings may damp off. Remove all dead leaves also. When the pots are filled with roots the plants should be fed once a week with Farmura. When the flower-buds appear in spring, water may be given freely.

Spring-sown annuals. These plants will be growing fairly vigorously from the seedling stage, so will need plenty of water, and should be grown in houses which are well ventilated. As soon as the flowering pots are comfortably filled with roots a weekly feed will be beneficial as for the autumn-sown plants.

Staking. The dwarf kinds will, of course, need no staking at all. Tall plants can be neatly staked and tied with raffia, while those of medium height are easily supported by twiggy stakes.

ALONSOA

Dwarf, half-hardy annual, 9–12 in. high, with scarlet or pink flowers. *A. warscewiczii compacta* is a scarlet, while *A. multisii* has pink flowers with deep crimson centres.

ANTIRRHINUM

Strictly a hardy perennial, but much use is made of it in pots. The colours range from white, through all shades of yellow, orange, pink and red to deep, almost black, velvety-red. The tall varieties grow about 3 ft high, and intermediate kinds from 15–18 in.

CLARKIA

These often attain 4 ft or more, when well grown in pots under glass. Large double flowers may be obtained in white and various shades of pink and red.

GODETIA

Hardy annuals with fairly large single or double flowers, white or various shades of pink, mauve or red. The taller varieties, growing about $3\frac{1}{2}$ ft high, are usually grown under glass.

LARKSPUR

The stock-flowered type, growing about 4–5 ft high, makes excellent pot plants. The flowers are double, and white, pale pink, salmon-pink, rosy-scarlet, mauve or blue in colour.

MIGNONETTE

Popular, sweetly scented flowers, growing 18 in. to 2 ft high. The best varieties include the machet and special pot kinds.

NEMESIA

Half-hardy annuals growing 9–12 in. high. Large-flowered varieties may be obtained in white, blue or various shades of yellow, orange, pink or red.

NICOTIANA

These plants with scented flowers may be grown in the shady part of the house and are especially fragrant in the evenings and early in the morning. *N. affinis* has large white flowers and grows about 3 ft high; there are also pink and red varieties. A dainty variety is *N. suaveolens* with smaller delicately scented white flowers.

PETUNIA

The large-flowered single and double varieties are most suitable for pot work. The flowers are elegant and coloured white, pink, red, pale blue, violet, or they may be striped with various colours.

PHACELIA CAMPANULARIA
A showy dwarf hardy annual with bright blue, bell-shaped flowers, blooming within six weeks of sowing.

RHODANTHE
Charming half-hardy annuals with white or pink daisy-like everlasting flowers. They only grow from 9–12 in. high.

SALPIGLOSSIS
Half-hardy annuals with large, ornamental, funnel-shaped flowers, delicately veined, and coloured brown and gold, blue and gold, red and gold, etc. They grow about 3 ft high.

SCABIOUS
Although really a biennial, the sweet scabious is normally treated as an annual. Growing about 3 ft high, the flowers may be white, cream, pink, red, mauve or deep purple.

SCHIZANTHUS
Sometimes called the Butterfly Flower, this half-hardy annual is a valuable pot plant. The flowers are very freely produced and may be coloured white or various shades of yellow, pink, crimson, mauve or purple.

STATICE
An everlasting flower that is very popular. There are various types, some like Sinuata which is rather stiff, and others like Suworowii which is 'wavy' and light. There are blues and whites, rose colours and purples.

STOCKS
The half-hardy annuals include the ordinary 10-week stocks and the Beauty of Nice strains. The East Lothian and Brompton stocks are really biennials, though are often treated as annuals. The flowers are coloured white, yellow, pink, apricot, blue, crimson, mauve or purple.

URSINIA
Half-hardy annuals from South Africa, only about 9 in. high, with orange flowers. The plants should be placed in a sunny

spot as the flowers tend to close up in dull weather, or towards evening.

WALLFLOWERS

Although really a perennial and normally treated as biennial, there are some double varieties, 9–18 in. high, which may be treated as annuals. If sown in July or August, they will flower early the following spring. Many beautiful colours may be obtained.

BROWALLIA

Very free-flowering plants with blue, violet or white tubular flowers. *Time of flowering* Winter or summer depending upon time of sowing. *Time of sowing* Spring for summer flowering in a temperature of 55–65°F, July for winter flowering. *Position* Pots. *Temperature* March to June 55–60°F. *Feeding* Feed once or twice a week when the pots are filled with roots and the flower buds appear. *General management* Pot off seedlings singly when they are large enough to handle, and pot on as they require it. Pinch back three or four times to encourage dwarf, bushy growth. The plants from the July sowing may be grown in a cold frame until the end of September. When inside the plants should be syringed daily.

CELOSIA (Cockscomb)

Decorative annuals with small flowers in feathery heads. *Time of flowering* Summer. *Time of sowing* March in a temperature of 65–70°F. *Position* Pots in full sunlight. *Temperature* 55–65°F. *Feeding* Feed once a week when the pots are filled with roots. *General management* When the seedlings are large enough, they should be potted on fairly firmly as they require it. Careful watering is essential but the foliage should be syringed twice a day and plenty of air should be given whenever the weather is suitable.

DIDISCUS (Blue Lace Flower)

A delightful pot plant, with heads of tiny blue flowers. *Time of flowering* July. *Time of sowing* February in a temperature of 55°F. *Position* Pots in the sun. *Temperature* 45–50°F. *General management* Pot off the seedlings singly as soon as they are large enough, and pot on immediately the pots are full of roots, 5- or 6-in. pots are usually used as finals, and the plants may be watered freely as soon as they are well established.

IMPATIENS (Balsam)

Plants 18–24 in. high with brightly coloured flowers. *Time of flowering* Summer and autumn. *Time of sowing* From the end of March till the beginning of May in a temperature of 60°F. *Position* In pots near the glass. No shading is necessary. *Temperature* 55–65°F. *Feeding* Feed two or three times a week when the pots are filled with roots. *General management* It is important to obtain seeds of a good strain from a reliable source. The seedlings should be potted off singly into small pots as soon as the first rough leaf appears. They must not be starved in the early stages, and should be potted on as soon as the roots touch the sides of the pots. No stopping is necessary. Plenty of water must be given, and the plants may be syringed frequently until the flowers begin to open. The flowering season will be prolonged if all blooms are removed immediately they wither.

11 Bulbs and corms

Apart from the tender bulbs and corms, which will be dealt with in the second part of this chapter, many of the hardy and half-hardy bulbous plants take very kindly to pot culture. If subjected to gentle forcing they may be had in flower some weeks earlier than those in the garden outside.

POTTING

Early potting is essential in order to be really successful with early flowers. Pots 5, 6 or 7 in. in diameter are the most useful sizes for the majority of the bulbs, though smaller ones may be used for such subjects as crocuses, scilla, etc., and larger ones for some of the lilies. August and September are the usual months for potting such common kinds as narcissus, tulips, hyacinths, crocuses, irises, etc., lilies, gladioli and tritonias may be started about November, or late gladioli in March or April.

The John Innes Potting Compost or Alex Soil-less Compost are excellent for all bulbs. The pots should have the usual crocks and rough material at the bottom, and the compost should be moist and pressed round the bulbs fairly firmly. The larger bulbs, except lilies and irises, usually have the tips just above the soil surface, but smaller kinds such as snowdrops and scillas can be buried just below the surface.

The pots should be stood outside on an ash or concrete base so that worms are prevented from entering through the holes in the bottom of the pots. They should then be covered with about 3 in. of old sifted ashes, sand or fibre and left for at least eight weeks. They will receive all the moisture they need from the rain draining through the covering material, and will be kept at a fairly even temperature, and protected from frost.

FORCING

At the end of eight weeks or so, the pots should be examined, and the most forward plants taken into the greenhouse, the remainder being brought in in batches to provide a succession

Greenhouse used for decorative plants with a garden frame on one side. Garden frames are easily moved from one part of a garden to another. CRITTALL WARMLIFE LTD.

An anchor leg, used to give a firm base when erecting a greenhouse. MARLEY GREENHOUSES

Preparing the base of a greenhouse. The aluminium frame is clipped to the anchor leg. MARLEY GREENHOUSES

Checking that the base of the house is square and level. MARLEY GREENHOUSES

A paraffin heater, perhaps the cheapest convenient greenhouse heating system. MARLEY GREENHOUSES

of flowers. They should then be put in a cool house at first, and not in full light; after a day or two they may receive all the light possible and a temperature of 60–70°F. Plenty of water should be given while they are growing, and the temperature should be reduced slightly as they come into flower.

AFTER FLOWERING

Bulbs are usually not suitable for forcing a second season, but are best planted out in a wild part of the garden where they will recover and establish themselves. If it is desired to keep any special ones, they should be stood beneath the staging and kept moist until the foliage dies down, then kept dry until time for repotting.

Tender bulbs and corms

Those mentioned under this heading also do quite well in the John Innes Potting Compost No. 2 or Alex Soil-less Compost.

CRINUM (Cape Lily)

Handsome deciduous, bulbous plants. The bulbs are large and the lily-like flowers are borne on stems from 2–3 ft high. The leaves are large and arching. *Time of flowering* April to October. *Propagation* (1) Offsets at potting time. (2) Seeds sown in spring in a temperature of 65–75°F. Seedlings take several years before flowering. *Position* Large, well-drained pots or tubs in a light part of the house. After flowering, stand outside until the autumn. *Temperature* March to September 55–65°F, September to March 45–50°F. *Feeding* Feed established plants once a week during the summer. *General management* Repot bulbs in March every three or four years. Water freely in spring and summer, but very sparingly for the rest of the year. Store the pots on their sides during the winter.

CYCLAMEN (Sowbread)

Deciduous perennial flowering plants. The foliage is often marbled and marked, and the flowers are white or various shades of pink, crimson or salmon-scarlet. *Time of flowering* Winter. *Propagation* Seeds sown $\frac{1}{4}$ in. deep from August to November or January to March in a temperature of 55°F. *Position* Pots in a cold frame from May to September, inside for the rest of the year but shaded from the sun. *Feeding*

Feed once a week when in flower. *General management* Repot
in July or August. The corm should always be partly above the
surface of the soil. Water moderately and syringe until new
growth begins, then freely until the plants have ceased to
flower, then keep almost dry from May to July. Best results are
obtained from one-year-old seedling plants.

EUCHARIS (Amazon Lily)
Evergreen bulbous plants, 1–2 ft high with white flowers.
Time of flowering December to March. *Propagation* (1) Offsets in
June or July. (2) Seeds sown in $\frac{1}{2}$ in. deep in February or
March in a temperature of 85°F. *Position* Well-drained pots.
Temperature March to September 70–80°F, December to
March 65–75°F. *Feeding* Feed twice a week after the flowering
stems appear. *General management* Repot firmly in June or July
every three or four years. Water freely in spring and summer,
moderately at other times. Syringe freely during the summer.
Top-dress established plants each March with a rich compost.

FREESIA
Dainty, well-known bulbous plants with fragrant flowers of
many colours. *Time of flowering* Winter and early spring.
Propagation (1) Offsets at potting time. (2) Seeds sown in cool
greenhouse or frame in March or April, or as soon as ripe.
Seedlings must not be repotted in their first year. May flower
within six months of sowing. *Position* Pots in cool house.
Temperature Never lower than 40°F. *Feeding* Feed once a week
when the flowers show. *General management* Repot each year in
August for January flowering, in October for February
flowering, in November for March flowering and in December
for April flowering. Bulbs should be put in 1 in. deep and 2 in.
apart. Stand in cool spot and give very little water until
growth starts, then water freely until plants have flowered.
Afterwards gradually decrease the supply and keep quite dry
until July.

HAEMANTHUS (Red Cape Tulip or Blood Lily)
Deciduous bulbous plants from South Africa. *Time of flowering*
Spring or summer. *Propagation* Offsets at potting time. *Position*
Well-drained pots exposed to full sun while growing; under
staging when at rest. *Temperature* March to September 55–65°F,
September to March 45–55°F. *Feeding* Feed once or twice a
week when in flower. *General management* Repot immediately

after flowering, but it is not advisable to disturb the roots too often. Pot up new bulbs in the autumn. Water very little till growth begins, then moderately till the plants finish flowering, and then freely as it is at this time that the bulbs make their annual growth. When the foliage has died down keep dry until growth starts again.

HIPPEASTRUM (Amaryllis, Barbados Lily)
Extremely showy bulbous plants. The leaves are long and strap-shaped and the flowers large and funnel-shaped, white or various shades of pink or red. *Time of flowering* Early spring to early summer. *Propagation* (1) Offsets at repotting time. (2) Seeds sown in March or as soon as they are ripe in a temperature of 65–70°F. Seedlings are 3–4 years old before they flower. *Position* Well-drained pots in a light part of the house. *Temperature* February to September 65–75°F, September to February 50–55°F. *Feeding* Feed once a week when the flower-spike shows. *General management* Repot every three or four years in January, burying the bulbs about two thirds of their depth. Water freely from the time when growth begins until July, afterwards keep quite dry. Top-dress bulbs each year if they are not repotted.

LACHENALIA (Cape Cowslip or Leopard Lily)
Deciduous, bulbous-rooted plants with flowers of orange, red or gold. Sometimes the leaves are spotted. Good for hanging baskets. *Time of flowering* January, February, March and early spring. *Propagation* Seed sown when ripe. Offsets taken from the parent plant, potted up in August. *Position* Cold frame until November, then transfer to a sunny shelf in the greenhouse. *Temperature* 55°F if flowers are wanted early. *Feeding* Feed as the flower buds appear with weak liquid manure. *General management* Water freely when growing well and dry off after flowering so that the bulbs may ripen during the summer months.

NERINE (Scarlet Guernsey Lily)
These are among the most beautiful bulbous plants suitable for greenhouse culture. The plants are deciduous and clusters of pink or red flowers are produced on stout stems 1–2 ft high. *Time of flowering* August to October. *Propagation* (1) Offsets at potting time; these may take several years before they reach flowering size. (2) Seeds sown in heat as soon as they are ripe.

Position Well-drained pots in a light house from September to May; cold frame in the sun for the rest of the year. *Temperature* 45–55°F. *Feeding* Feed occasionally during the growing period. *General management* Pot August to November. Top-dress with fresh compost each year in August, since repotting is only necessary every three or four years. Water moderately until the flower-spikes show, but keep quite dry during the summer.

ORNITHOGALUM (Arabian Star of Bethlehem)

One species is commonly grown in greenhouses. The flowers are white and fragrant, with black centres, and borne several together in a head on 18-in. stems. *Time of flowering* Summer. *Propagation* Offsets removed from September to February. *Position* Well-drained pots in the sun. *Temperature* March to September 55–65°F, September to March 40–50°F. *Feeding* Feed occasionally when growing vigorously. *General management* Repot each year any time between September and February. Water moderately until growing strongly, then freely. Withhold water gradually as leaves turn yellow, then keep dry until bulbs are repotted.

VALLOTA (Scarborough Lily)

A bulbous plant rather similar to a small hippeastrum. The stems are 2–3 ft high, bearing scarlet flowers. *Time of flowering* August and September. *Propagation* Offsets removed at potting time. *Position* Well-drained pots in light house August to May, outside in a sunny frame for the rest of the year. *Temperature* September to March 40–50°F, March to May 55–65°F. *Feeding* Feed once or twice a week from March to June. *General management* Pot up firmly in June or July. Repotting is only necessary every three or four years. Pot up new bulbs in October, November, March or April. Water moderately September to March; freely March to June, and keep dry for the rest of the year.

12 Flowering plants

There are so many herbaceous flowering plants which may be grown in a greenhouse, that it is impossible to deal with them all. Those mentioned in this chapter are all fairly easy to grow, some more so than others, and there are none which cannot be obtained from one of the nurseries supplying greenhouse plants.

Some also have ornamental foliage or berries, but are included here mainly on account of their flowers.

(Composts and feeding as at the beginning of Chapter 13.)

ACHIMENES
Tuberous-rooted perennials growing 12–18 in. high. Flowers red, blue, purple or white. *Time of flowering* June to October. *Propagation* (1) Division of the tubers in February. (2) Cuttings of young shoots and leaves in April. (3) Seeds sown $\frac{3}{4}$ in. deep in a temperature of 70–80°F in March. *Position* In shallow pans or hanging baskets, shaded from strong sunshine. *Temperature* Until flowering, the temperature should be maintained at about 60–65°F after which it may be reduced slightly, but must not fall below 50°F. *Feeding* Feed once a week as soon as the pots are filled with roots. *General management* To obtain a succession of flowers, the tubers are started into growth at intervals from February to the beginning of May. They are potted up moderately firmly, 2 or 3 in. apart, and placed on shelves near the glass. They like a moist atmosphere and water is given sparingly at first, but freely later when the plants are growing strongly. After flowering, water is gradually withheld, and when the stems have dried off the pots are stored on their sides until the following spring. *Pests* Red spider may be troublesome if the atmosphere is allowed to become too dry. Aphides may be kept down by fumigation. Thrips by regular sprayings with nicotine.

AECHMEA
Plants with rather stiff leaves forming a rosette and yellow, blue or red flowers. *Time of flowering* July and August. *Propaga-*

tion Offsets at any time. *Position* Well-drained pots. *Temperature*
March to September 70–80°F, September to March 60–65°F.
General management Repot in March. Water freely.

AESCHYANTHUS (Blush-Wort)

Evergreen hairy trailing plants, with broad, toothed leaves,
and scarlet tubular flowers with a yellow throat. *Time of
flowering* June. *Propagation* Cuttings of firm shoots, 3 in. long in
February in a temperature of 85°F. *Compost* Equal parts of
fibrous peat, sphagnum moss and charcoal. *Position* Pots or
baskets. *Temperature* March to September 70–80°F, September
to March 60–65°F. *General management* Repot in March. Water
freely in summer, moderately in winter.

AGAPANTHUS (African Lily)

Leaves grow up from the base of the plant, and are long,
narrow and evergreen. Blue or white tubular flowers produced
in a head on a stem about 3 ft long. *Time of flowering* May and
June. *Propagation* Division in March. *Position* Large pots or
tubs in the sun. *Temperature* March to September 45–55°F,
September to March, 32–40°F. *Feeding* The plants are heavy
feeders and should be fed frequently during their growing
period. *General management* They dislike root disturbance and
will not flower freely if repotted too often. When it is necessary,
they should be repotted in March. Water is given freely during
the growing season, and sparingly in winter.

AGATHAEA (Blue Marguerite, Cape Aster)

A small shrubby, herbaceous perennial otherwise called Felicia
with heads of sky-blue, daisy-like flowers. *Time of flowering* May
to September. *Propagation* (1) Cuttings of young shoots in
March or August in a temperature of 55–65°F. (2) Seeds sown
in spring or summer in a temperature of 60–65°F. *Position* Pots
in the sun. *Temperature* 45–55°F. *General management* Seedlings
should be potted off singly, fairly firmly and pinched two or
three times to encourage bushy growth. Plants for flowering in
late summer may be put out in a cold frame during the early
summer months.

AGLAONEMA (Poison Dart)

Dwarf plant with arum-shaped flowers and leaves variegated
with grey. *Time of flowering* July. *Propagation* Division of roots
in March. *Position* Well-drained pots in the shade. *Temperature*

March to September 70–80°F, September to March 60–65°F.
General management Repot in March. Water freely during the
growing season, sparingly at other times. Syringe the leaves
once a day.

ALPINIA (Indian Shell-flower)

Plants with showy flowers, and often with ornamental leaves.
Time of flowering Spring or summer. *Propagation* Division of
roots in March. *Position* Large pots, tubs or beds. *Temperature*
March to September 70–80°F, September to March 55–65°F.
General management Pot or plant in March. Water freely in
summer, moderately at other times.

AMASONIA

Evergreen flowering plant. *Time of flowering* September. *Propagation* Division of plants in March. *Position* Small pots well
exposed to light, but shaded from strong sunlight. *Temperature*
March to September 70–85°F, September to March 58–65°F.
General management Repot in March. Water freely in spring and
summer, moderately at other times.

ANTHURIUM (Flamingo-plant, Tail-flower)

Plants with ornamental foliage and brightly coloured flowers
on long stems. The flowers are flat, with a thick spike in the
centre. *Time of flowering* March to August. *Propagation* (1) Division of roots in March. (2) Seeds sown in spring in a temperature of 80°F in a compost consisting of chopped sphagnum
moss, charcoal and sand. *Compost* Equal parts of rough peat
and sphagnum moss. *Position* Well-drained pots shaded from
bright sunlight. *Temperature* March to September 70–80°F,
September to March 60–65°F. *Humidity* A moist atmosphere is
essential. *General management* Repot in March. Water freely in
spring and summer, but moderately at other times.

ASCLEPIAS (Swallow-wort, Milkweed, Silkweed)

Plant growing about 3 ft high, the leaves are oblong, and the
flowers reddish-purple with orange hoods are borne in large
erect clusters. *Time of flowering* July to September. *Propagation*
(1) Division of the roots in October or April. (2) Cuttings in
spring in a propagating frame or under a 4-sided cloche.
(3) Seeds sown in gentle heat in February in a temperature of
50–60°F. The resulting seedlings should flower the same year.
Position Pots on the sunny side of a warm house. *Temperature*

Winter temperature must be at least 60–65°F. *General management* Repot in spring and cut back growths. Plants should be kept rather dry during the winter.

ATACCIA
Perennial with large, shiny, purplish-green leaves, and brownish-purple flowers. *Time of flowering* Summer. *Position* Well-drained pots. *Temperature* March to September 75–85°F, September to March 60–65°F. *General management* Repot in February or March. Water freely in summer, sparingly at other times.

BEGONIAS
A large genus of tuberous and fibrous-rooted perennials. The tuberous section is more popular, the large flowers may be single or double, and sometimes frilled, in white and various shades of yellow, orange, pink and red.

Begonias and chlorophytum growing happily together in a bowl

The fibrous-rooted group make larger plants on the whole, while the individual flowers are smaller, and white, pink or red in colour. Some species are grown for their ornamental foliage.

TUBEROUS ROOTED SECTION

Time of flowering Summer and autumn. *Propagation* (1) Cuttings of young shoots in spring. (2) Seeds down in a temperature of 65–75°F in February to April. *Position* In pots shaded from direct sunlight. *Temperature* 65–70°F during growing season, 50–55°F during winter. *Feeding* Feed about once a week when growth is active. *General management* The tubers are started into growth in February or March by planting in boxes of sterilized soil or peat-moss or leaf-mould in heat. As soon as they are rooted pot up into small pots and pot on later as they require it. Flower buds should be picked off until the plants are well established. Water is given sparingly at first, but freely when the plants are growing strongly. After flowering, water is gradually withheld until the tops have dried off, the pots are then stored on their sides during the winter.

FIBROUS ROOTED SECTION

Time of flowering Autumn, winter and early spring. *Propagation* (1) Leaf cuttings in spring or summer (2) Shoot cuttings in February or March. (3) Seeds sown in January to February in a temperature of 65–75°F. *Compost* Pulled peat, pulled loam, charcoal and sand. *Position* In pots shaded from sun. *Temperature* 55°F in autumn and winter, 55–65°F in spring and summer. *Feeding* Feed occasionally during the growing season. *General management* Keep moist during early stages of growth and syringe plants daily; in autumn, air should be kept drier and water given sparingly. After flowering, gradually withhold water and keep rather dry until March. Repot in March when necessary.

BILLBERGIA

Evergreen plants with leaves in rosettes or clusters. *Time of flowering* Spring. *Propagation* Large offsets in April in a temperature of 85°F. *Position* Well-drained pots in warm house. *Temperature* March to September 70–80°F, September to March 60–65°F. *General management* Repot in March. Water freely at all times.

CALCEOLARIA (Slipper-flower, Slipper-wort)

Plants growing from 1–3 ft high, bearing spreading heads of large, gaily coloured flowers marked with blotches and spots. They may be divided into herbaceous species and shrubby species.

HERBACEOUS SPECIES

Time of flowering May to October. *Propagation* Seeds sown in July. *Position* Pots shaded from bright sunlight. *Temperature* August to March 45–50°F, March to October 50–55°F. *Feeding* Feed once a week from April till the plants come into flower. *General management* Pot up young plants when large enough to handle, and pot on as they require it. Water moderately till April, then freely. Plants may be thrown away after flowering.

SHRUBBY SPECIES

Time of flowering Summer. *Propagation* (1) Cuttings of shoots 3 in. long in cold frame in September or October. (2) Seeds sown in March in a temperature of 50–60°F. *Position* Pots shaded from strong sunlight. *Temperature* Winter 45–50°F, Summer 50–55°F. *Feeding* Established plants should be fed once a week. *General management* Pot on young plants as they require it, and pinch back once or twice to produce bushy growth. Repot in March, and cut back into shape. The soil should always be kept moist.

CAMPANULA
Although this genus is chiefly grown in the open, there are some species which are suited to pot culture. Flowers are blue, mauve or white, and bell-shaped. *Time of flowering* June and July. *Propagation* (1) Basal cuttings of *C. isophylla* in warm temperature. (2) Seeds sown in a temperature of 55°F in March or August. *Position* Pots or baskets for *C. isophylla*. *Temperature* 45–55°F. *Feeding* Feed once a week when the flower-spikes begin to show. *General management* Repot if necessary in March. Plants should be watered moderately in winter and freely in summer.

CANNA (Indian Shot-Plant)
Plants with large, broad leaves and brightly coloured flowers, growing from 2–6 ft high. *Time of flowering* Summer. *Propagation* (1) Division of roots at potting time. (2) Seeds sown 1 in. deep in a temperature of 85°F in February or March. Before sowing, the seeds should be soaked in tepid water for 24 hours; filing a slight notch in the seed will also facilitate germination. *Position* Pots in the sun. *Temperature* 60°F during the growing season; may be used in the summer for subtropical bedding outside. *Feeding* Feed once or twice a week during the growing

season. *General management* Plants should be started into growth in March, when they can be repotted. Water should be given freely during the growing season. After flowering, growth ceases, so the plants should be dried off gradually, then stored for winter in a frost-proof shed, or beneath the greenhouse staging.

Cineraria multiflora

CELSIA (Cretan Mullein)

A biennial growing 4–5 ft high. The flower-spike is very like that of a mullein, bearing large, soft yellow flowers, each blossom being marked with velvety-brown spots at the base of the upper petals. *Time of flowering* June to September. *Propagation* Seeds sown in pots and germinated in cold frame, in early spring for autumn flowering, or in July or August for flowering the following summer. *Position* Light and well ventilated. *Temperature* 45–50°F. *Feeding* Feed once a week when the pots are filled with roots. *General management* Water moderately during the young stages of growth, but freely as soon as the plants have received their final potting.

CINERARIA (sometimes called Senecio)
Perennials, 1–2 ft high with fairly large leaves, and heads of daisy-like flowers varying in colour from white through pink and red to mauve and blue. Usually grown as annuals. *Time of flowering* December to May. *Propagation* (1) Cuttings in spring or early summer. (2) Seeds sown in April to July in a temperature of 65–75°F. *Position* Pots in cold frame from July till October, in cool house, in winter and spring. Should be shaded from strong sunlight. *Temperature* 45–50°F. *Feeding* Feed twice a week from September onwards. *General management* Pot up seedlings when large enough and pot on fairly firmly into larger pots as it becomes necessary. Always keep the soil moist. Need very careful watering.

CLIVIA (Kaffir Lily)
Fleshy-rooted plants with long, narrow, evergreen leaves and showy heads of short, tubular flowers in varying shades of scarlet, orange and yellow, on stems about 2 ft high. *Time of flowering* December to July. *Propagation* (1) Division of roots at potting time. (2) Seeds sown in temperature of 75°F in March. *Position* In pots in the sun and as close to the glass as possible. *Temperature* March to September 60–65°F, September to March 45–55°F. *Feeding* Well-established plants should be fed once a week. *General management* Plants should be watered and ventilated freely from March to September, and moderately for the rest of the year. They flower better when slightly pot-bound, but when repotting is necessary it should be carried out in February. Seedlings must never be dried off until after they have flowered.

CRYPTANTHUS
Evergreen plants with flattened rosettes of stiff, prickly leaves. *Time of flowering* Summer. *Propagation* Large offsets in April in a temperature of 85°F. *Position* Well-drained pots. *Temperature* March to September 75–85°F, September to March 60–65°F. *General management* Repot in March. Water freely at all times.

CUPHEA (Mexican Cigar Flower)
Dwarf evergreen plant with bright scarlet tubular flowers. *Time of flowering* June to August. *Propagation* (1) Cuttings of

young shoots in a temperature of 65–75°F. (2) Seeds sown in
same temperature in March. *Position* Pots near the glass. Does
well in hanging baskets. *Temperature* March to September
60–70°F, September to March 50–55°F. *Feeding* Feed once a
week as soon as the pots are comfortably full of roots. *General
management* Pot in March or April; they should be made fairly
firm at the final potting. Pinch the shoots to encourage bushy
growth, and cut back in January. Water freely during growing
season, but after flowering, plants must be kept fairly dry.
Syringe daily on bright days until the flowers form.

DESMODIUM (Telegraph Plant)
Perennial, 2–3 ft high, with small violet or purple flowers and
pinnate leaves, the leaflets of which move in all directions,
especially in the sun. *Time of flowering* July. *Propagation* (1)
Cuttings in March or April in a temperature of 75–80°F.
(2) Seeds sown in February or March in a similar temperature.
Position Well-drained pots. *Temperature* March to September
65–75°F, September to March 55–65°F. *General management*
Repot in February or March. Water moderately in winter,
freely at other times.

DICENTRA (Chinaman's Breeches, Bleeding Heart)
(sometimes called Dielytra)
Hardy perennial which responds to gentle forcing. Fern-like
foliage and graceful racemes of rosy-crimson or white flowers.
Time of flowering Spring and early summer. *Propagation* Division
of roots in autumn or spring. *Position* Pots in warm house, cold
frame from October to January. *Temperature* 55–65°F January
till after flowering. *General management* Roots are potted up in
October. Plenty of water should be given during growth. After
flowering, the plants may be put outside again since they are
of no more use for pot work.

DIONAEA (Venus' Fly Trap)
Insectivorous plant. The leaves are two-lobed, margined with
teeth and sensitive, the two lobes close together when touched.
Small white flowers are borne in a head 6 to 12 in. high.
Time of flowering July and August. *Propagation* (1) Division
of plants in March. (2) Seeds sown in March or April in a
mixture of sphagnum moss and peat under a bellglass.
Compost Equal parts of peat and living sphagnum moss.
Position Well-drained pots or pans, standing in about 1 in. of

water. *Temperature* March to September 45–50°F, September to March 40–45°F. *General management* Repot in March or April. Water freely at all times. The atmosphere may be kept moist by placing the pots under bell-glasses.

DROSERA (Sundew, Youth-Wort)

Insectivorous plants with small, white, pink or red flowers, and leaves covered with glandular hairs, which fold over when touched. *Time of flowering* June to September. *Propagation* (1) Division of the plants in March or April. (2) Cuttings of roots ½–1 in. long in a temperature of 65–75°F. (3) Seeds sown on the surface of living sphagnum moss and peat in a temperature of 55–65°F at any time. *Compost* Equal parts living sphagnum moss and sedge peat. *Position* Well-drained pots standing in a pan of water and covered with a bell-glass. *Temperature* 45–50°F. *General management* Repot in March or April. Water freely at all times.

ERANTHEMUM

Flowering plants with ornamental foliage. *Time of flowering* Spring and summer. *Propagation* Cuttings of young shoots from March to July in a temperature of 75°F. *Position* Well-drained pots in a light house from September to June, in a cold frame June to September. *Temperature* September to March 55–65°F, March to June 65–75°F. *Feeding* Feed occasionally when the plants are in flower. *General management* Repot in March or April. Water moderately in winter, freely at other times. Cut shoots back to within 1 in. of their base after flowering.

FRANCOA (Maiden's Wreath, Bridal Wreath)

Plants 2–3 ft high, flowers white in dense spikes. *Time of flowering* July and August. *Propagation* (1) Division of plants at potting time. (2) Cuttings of shoots in summer. (3) Seeds sown under bell-glass in a temperature of 50–55°F in February, March or April. *Position* Well-drained pots. *Temperature* April to September 55–65°F, October to April 40–50°F. *Feeding* Feed well-rooted plants once or twice a week. *General management* Repot in March or April, but plants are not much use after three or four years. They need plenty of water in summer, but little in winter.

GERBERA (Barberton or Transvaal Daisy)

Plants with daisy-like flowers borne singly on stems to 15 in.

high. *Time of flowering* June to October. *Propagation* (1) Cuttings of side-shoots in spring. (2) Seeds sown in March in a temperature of 55°F. Be sure to sow the seeds *on end* and never lying flat, as in the latter position they damp off. *Position* Pots in the sun. *Temperature* 45–50°F. *General management* Repot each year in spring. Water sparingly from November to April, freely at other times.

GESNERA

Tuberous-rooted flowering plants with ornamental velvety foliage. *Time of flowering* Summer to winter. *Propagation* (1) Cuttings of young shoots in spring in a temperature of 75–85°F. (2) Mature leaf-cuttings in similar temperature. (3) Seeds sown in March or April in a temperature of 75°F. *Compost* 2 of peat, 1 of fibrous loam (pulled to pieces), $\frac{1}{2}$ of sand and a handful of charcoal. *Position* Well-drained pots or pans in the shade. *Temperature* March to September 75–85°F, September to March 45–55°F. *Feeding* Feed once a week when the flower buds show, but on the whole little feeding is needed. *General management* Pot up the tubers 1 in. deep in March for summer flowering, May for autumn flowering and June for winter flowering. Water moderately till plants are 3–4 in. high, then freely. After flowering gradually withhold water till the leaves die down, then keep dry until repotting time, storing the pots on their sides.

GLOXINIA

Tuberous-rooted plants with large, bell-shaped flowers of various colours. The leaves are large and heavy and almost stemless. *Time of flowering* Autumn. *Propagation* (1) Cuttings of shoots 1–2 in. long inserted in small pots under a bell-glass in a temperature of 65–75°F. (2) Cuttings of leaves in a temperature of 55–75°F. (3) Seeds in March in a temperature of 65–75°F. *Position* Well-drained pots close to the glass in the shady side of the house. *Temperature* January to October 65–75°F, October to January 50–55°F. *Feeding* Feed once a week when the flower buds appear. *General management* Pot up tubers in January, February or March, singly in 3- or 4-in. pots, and potting on into larger pots as soon as the tubers have started growing. The soil should be made fairly firm, and the corm not quite buried. During the first stages of growth, water should be given sparingly, but more freely when the plants are growing vigorously. The plants should only be watered when

Dobie's new Gloxinia Hybrid 'Colour Palette'

they really need it. After flowering water should be withheld gradually until the leaves dry off and the plants then kept dry until the following spring. *Pests* The plants should be kept scrupulously clean, because flowers and leaves are susceptible to attack by thrips, which are very difficult to eradicate.

HEDYCHIUM (Fragrant Garland Flower)

Plants growing 3–5 ft high. The large leaves are ornamental and the flowers fragrant. *Time of growing* Summer. *Propagation* Division of roots in March or April. *Position* Large well-drained pots, tubs or boxes or in the borders of the house. *Temperature* March to November 55–56°F, November to March 45–50°F. *Feeding* Feed once a week when in flower. *General management* Repot in March, water freely when the plants are in full growth, but after flowering, cut down the flower stems and keep rather on the dry side. The plants may be put outside during July and August.

HUMEA (Amaranth Feathers)

A biennial, growing 4–6 ft high with scented leaves and drooping, feathery sprays of pinkish-brown flowers. *Time of flowering* June to October. *Propagation* Seeds sown any time from April to July in pans in a cold frame or greenhouse. The seedlings are potted up singly into small pots when large enough to handle. *Position* Well-drained pots in a cold frame or outside supported by stakes like chrysanthemums during the summer, in a well-ventilated house in winter and when in flower. Shade from very bright sunlight. *Temperature* April to October 55–65°F, October to April 45–55°F. *Feeding* Feed once a week when the flower-spikes show. *General management* Pot the seedlings on into larger pots as they require it. The plants should flower in 9- or 10-in. pots. Water must be given carefully at all times, and only enough to keep the plants alive is necessary in winter. Over-watering may cause the plants to die off suddenly. After flowering the plants are of no more use.

Humea may cause a rash on some people.

JACOBINIA
Perennials with tubular, two-lipped, orange, red or yellow flowers. *Time of flowering* Summer or winter. *Propagation* Cuttings of young shoots from March to July in a temperature of 75°F. *Position* Well-drained pots in sunny frame from June to September, in house for remainder of year. *Temperature* September to March 45–55°F, March to June 65–75°F. *Feeding* Feed twice a week when in flower. *General management* Repot in March or April. Water moderately from September to March, freely at other times. Cut back shoots to within 1 in. of their base after flowering. Young shoots should be pinched back occasionally during the summer to induce bushy growth.

JUSTICIA
Plants with ornamental foliage and flowers very similar to those of Jacobinia. *Time of flowering* Winter. For details of cultivation and propagation, see Jacobinia.

LOTUS
Shrubby plant, growing about 2 ft high, with silvery leaves and small scarlet flowers. *Time of flowering* Summer. *Propagation* (1) Cuttings of shoots in summer in a temperature of 55–65°F. (2) Seeds sown in March or April in a temperature of 55–65°F. *Position* Pots in the sun. *Temperature* March to September 55–65°F, September to March 45–55°F. *Feeding* Feed plants once a week when in flower. *General management* Repot in February or March. Give plenty of ventilation when weather is suitable. Water moderately in summer, very sparingly in winter.

MARGUERITE (Chrysanthemum frutescens)

The white, daisy-flowered Marguerite is useful for flowering in pots. *Time of flowering* Summer. *Propagation* Cuttings of firm young shoots in April, singly in a thumb pot or 3 or 4 in a 3-in. pot. *Position* Outside in full sunlight from July to September, in a cold frame until November and then in a heated house. *Temperature* 50–55°F. *Feeding* Feed well-established plants once a week. *General management* When the cuttings are rooted they are potted off singly into small pots and potted on into larger sizes as they require it. They should be pinched back two or three times to produce bushy plants. Plenty of water is needed while the plants are growing. *Pests and diseases* Aphides may be killed by fumigation or by spraying with Derris. The grubs of the chrysanthemum leaf-miner are often troublesome, especially during hot weather. Attacked leaves should be removed and burnt, and the plants sprayed with a nicotine wash.

MIMULUS (Musk)

Perennials with yellow or red tubular flowers. *Time of flowering* Summer. *Propagation* (1) Division of plants in March. (2) Cuttings of shoots, 2 in. long in a temperature of 55–65°F in March. (3) Seeds sown in a temperature of 55–60°F from February to May. *Position* Pots in a shady part of the house. *Temperature* March to October 50–65°F, October to March 40–50°F. *Feeding* Feed once a week when the pots are filled with roots. *General management* Potting may be done from February to April. Water is given freely from March to October. The quantity is then gradually reduced and the plants are kept almost dry after December. Plants not inclined to be bushy should be pinched back to make them so.

MOSCHOSMA

A perennial growing 2–3 ft high with nettle-like leaves and white and purplish flowers. *Time of flowering* Autumn and winter. *Propagation* Cuttings of young shoots in a temperature of 65°F in March. *Position* In pots in a cold frame from June to September inside for the remainder of the year. *Temperature* March to June 55–65°F, September to March 45–55°F. *Feeding* Feed once a week after the final potting in July. *General management* Shake the old soil from the roots in March and repot. Water freely from March to October, then moderately. After flowering, shoots should be cut back to within 3 in. of the base of the plant.

NERTERA (Coral Plant, Fruiting Duckweed)

A creeping perennial with round, bright orange-red or crimson berries. *Propagation* (1) Division of plants in March or April. (2) Seeds sown in March or April in a temperature of 55–65°F. *Position* Small, well-drained pots or pans in shade. *Temperature* March to October 50–60°F, October to March 40–50°F. *General management* Repot in February or March. Water freely in spring and summer, moderately at other times.

OPHIOPOGON (Japanese Hyacinth, Snake's Beard)

Perennial growing about 1 ft high. The leaves are long and narrow and margined with white. The flowers are borne on slender spikes and are white in colour. *Time of flowering* July. *Propagation* Division of plants in February and March. *Position* Well-drained pots or small beds in sun or shade. *Temperature* 40–45°F. *Feeding* Feed established plants once or twice a week during the growing season. *General management* Repot when necessary or plant in February or March. Plenty of water is needed from March to October, but little during the winter. Syringe once a day during hot weather.

OXALIS (Wood Sorrel)

Tuberous-rooted plants with clover-shaped leaves and various coloured flowers. By selection of suitable species plants may be had in flower for the greater part of the year. *Time of flowering* Spring and summer. *Propagation* (1) Division of roots at potting time. (2) Offsets at potting time. (3) Seeds sown in spring in a temperature of 55–65°F. *Position* Well-drained pots or baskets in the sun. *Temperature* 40–45°F. *Feeding* Feed established plants occasionally when growing actively. *General management* Spring-flowering species should be planted in January or February, and summer-flowering species in March or April. The roots should be planted $\frac{1}{2}$ in. deep, watered sparingly until the leaves start to grow, and then freely. After flowering, water should be reduced gradually until the leaves have quite died down, then keep dry until time for repotting.

PAVONIA

Evergreen flowering plants. *Time of flowering* Autumn. *Propagation* Cuttings at any time in a temperature of 75°F. *Position* Pots in shade. *Temperature* March to September 65–75°F,

September to March 45–55°F. *General management* Repot in March. Water freely in spring and summer, sparingly at other times. Syringe once a day during summer.

PELARGONIUM
Several types may be grown in pots; the leaves may be green or variegated, and the flowers borne in heads are of various colours.

SHOW PELARGONIUMS
Time of flowering Spring and early summer. *Propagation* Cuttings of firm shoots 2–2½ in. long in July or August in a cold frame. *Position* In pots, near the glass. Outside in the sun after flowering until September. *Temperature* September to March 45–50°F, March to May 50–55°F. *Feeding* Feed well-rooted plants twice a week until the flowers begin to open. *General management* Pot on rooted cuttings firmly as they require it and pinch back once or twice to encourage bushy growth. Repot old plants in August or September. Water freely from March to June, moderately at other times. Cut back shoots to within 1 in. of their base in July.

ZONAL PELARGONIUMS
Time of flowering These may be timed to bloom at any season of the year. *Propagation* (1) Cuttings of firm shoots in August or September in a temperature of 45°F for summer flowering; in February or March, in a temperature of 55–65°F for winter flowering. (2) Seeds sown from February to April in a temperature of 55–65°F. *Position* Pots shaded from the sun when in bloom. Winter flowering plants may be stood in a sunny cold frame from June to September. *Temperature* August to March 40–50°F, March to May 55–60°F (for summer flowering plants), September to March 50–55°F (for winter flowering plants). *Feeding* Feed twice a week when plants are well-established in their final pots. *General management* Pot on rooted cuttings firmly as they require it, and pinch back young shoots occasionally to encourage bushy growth. Repot old plants after flowering and cut back flowering shoots. Water moderately at all times.

IVY-LEAVED PELARGONIUMS
Time of flowering Summer. *Propagation* Cuttings in August or September. *Position* Pots or baskets. *Temperature* March to September 50–60°F, September to March 40–50°F. *Feeding* Feed twice a week when plants are well-established in their

final pots. *General management* Pot on rooted cuttings as they require it, pinching back the young shoots to induce bushy growth. Cut back plants in February or March, and repot. Water freely in summer, moderately at other times.

PHORMIUM (Common Flax Lily, New Zealand Flax)

Flowering plants with ornamental leaves. *Time of flowering* Summer. *Propagation* (1) Division of roots in April. (2) Seeds sown in March. *Position* Pots, tubs or beds; outside in the sun from June to September. *Temperature* 45–50°F. *General management* Repot in February through to April. Water copiously in summer, moderately at other times.

PRIMULA

Leaves in rosettes and single or double flowers in heads. *Time of flowering* Winter and spring. *Propagation* (1) Division of plants in case of *P. floribunda*, *P. verticillata* and double-flowered varieties. (2) Cuttings of young shoots after flowering in the case of double-flowered varieties. (3) Seeds sown in March or April. *Position* Pots in shady part of house. *Temperature* 50–55°F during growing season, 55–60°F during flowering season. *Feeding* Feed once a week when pots are filled with roots till the flowers begin to open. *General management* Young plants should be potted on as they require it, but not too firmly. The plants are rather apt to flop about, and this difficulty may be overcome by potting rather deeply. Roots will form from the bases of the lower leaves, thus giving extra support to the plant. Plenty of ventilation should be given and soil should be kept moist, although over-watering must be avoided, otherwise the leaves quickly turn yellow. Remove any early flower-buds.

PYCNOSTACHYS

Perennial with spikes of blue two-lipped flowers. *Time of flowering* Winter. *Propagation* (1) Division in spring. (2) Seeds sown in spring in a temperature of 65°F. *Position* Well-drained pots in the sun. *Temperature* March to September 60–65°F, September to March 45–55°F. *General management* Repot in spring. Water freely during the growing season, sparingly at other times.

REHMANNIA

Flowers are large, tubular and drooping and shaped rather like those of a foxglove. *Time of flowering* Spring and summer.

Propagation (1) Division of the plants in March. (2) Seeds sown in February and March in warm house. *Position* Well-drained pots shaded from strong sunlight. *Temperature* 40–45°F. *Feeding* Feed once a week when the pots are filled with roots. *General management* Old plants should be repotted in February or March. Plenty of water is needed during the growing season, but keep almost dry in winter.

REINECKEA
Perennial with creeping roots and long, narrow leaves and fragrant pink flowers. *Time of flowering* April. *Propagation* Division of roots in March or April. *Position* Pots in the sun. *Temperature* 45–50°F. *General management* Repot in March or April. Water copiously in summer, moderately at other times.

RICHARDIA (Arum or Calla Lily, Lily of the Nile)
In addition to the white Arum Lily which is well known, there are also species with yellow flowers, and some have variegated leaves. *Time of flowering* Winter, spring and early summer. *Propagation* (1) Division of tuberous roots in August or September. (2) Offsets in August or September. (3) Seeds sown in spring in temperature of 65–75°F. *Position* In large pots in house from October to May. Outside for the rest of the year. *Temperature* October to March 40–55°F, March to May 50–60°F. *Feeding* Feed once a week when pots are filled with roots. *General management* The plants are repotted in August, the old soil being shaken from the roots, which are planted up in new compost. Any damaged portions of the tubers must be cut away and the cut ends dusted with lime or charcoal. The pots must be brought inside before the early frosts start. During the growing season the roots are kept moist, but after flowering, the plants are gradually dried off and are stored on their sides until ready for repotting. *Pests and diseases* Aphides are often troublesome, but can easily be kept down by fumigation, or spraying with Derris.

RUELLA (Christmas Pride)
Flowering plants with funnel-shaped flowers. *Time of flowering* Winter. *Propagation* (1) Cuttings in spring or summer in temperature of 75–85°F. (2) Seeds sown in February or March in temperature of 70–75°F. *Position* Pots in the shade. *Temperature* March to September 65–75°F, September to March 55–65°F. *Feeding* Feed once a week during the flowering period. *General*

management Repot in February or March. Water freely in spring and summer, moderately at other times. Syringe twice a day in spring and summer, once a day for the rest of the year.

SAINTPAULIA (African Violet)

Perennial with fleshy, hairy leaves and deep-violet flowers with yellow stamens. *Time of flowering* August to March. *Propagation* (1) Leaf cuttings. (2) Seeds sown in spring in temperature of 60–65°F. *Position* Pots near the glass, but shaded from strong sunlight. *Temperature* April to October 65–75°F, October to April 45–55°F. *Feeding* Feed occasionally during the flowering season. *General management* Repot February to May. Watering must be done carefully, otherwise the plants may rot off.

SALVIA

Useful perennials, especially for small houses, and are easy to grow. *Time of flowering* Autumn and early winter. *Propagation* (1) Cuttings of shoots about 3 in. long in February or March in temperature of 65°F. (2) Seeds sown in March in a temperature of 60–65°F. *Position* Pots in cold frame, June to September, afterwards in a warm house. *Temperature* September to March 45–55°F, March to June 55–65°F. *Feeding* Feed well-rooted plants once or twice a week when they are in their final pots. *General management* Repot in March. Water freely during the spring and summer but sparingly in winter. After flowering cut down shoots to within 3 in. of their base. Young plants should be potted on as required and pinched once or twice to make bushy.

SARRACENIA (Huntsman's Horn, Indian Cup,
N. American Pitcher-Plant)

Insectivorous plant, with tubular, pitcher-shaped leaves. *Time of flowering* Spring and summer. *Propagation* Division in March or April. *Compost* Equal part fibrous peat and chopped sphagnum moss. *Position* Well-drained pots in cool moist house, shaded from bright sunlight. *Temperature* 45–50°F. *General management* Repot in March. Water freely in spring and summer, but very sparingly in winter. Syringe once a day in summer. Top-dress in summer with a little properly prepared vegetable compost.

SONERILA

Flowering plants with ornamental foliage. The leaves are green or spotted with silvery-white. *Time of flowering* Summer. *Propa-*

gation (1) Cuttings from January to May in a temperature of 75–85°F. (2) Seeds sown from January to April in a similar temperature. *Position* Well-drained pots or pans fully exposed to the light, but shaded from the strong sun. *Temperature* March to September 70–85°F, September to March 55–65°F. *General management* Repot in February or March. Water freely in summer, moderately at other times. A moist atmosphere is essential.

STATICE (Sea Lavender) (often called Limonium)
One perennial species is suitable for growing in the greenhouse. Annual species are dealt with in Chapter 10. *Time of flowering* Summer. *Propagation* Heel cuttings of side-shoots in spring in a temperature of 70°F with a little bottom heat. *Position* Pots in a cold frame May to September and in a sunny well-ventilated house for the rest of the year. *Temperature* September to April 40–50°F, April to May 55–65°F. *Feeding* Feed established plants occasionally during the summer, using Farmura. *General management* Repot in spring. Give plenty of water when the plants are in full growth, otherwise only just enough to keep the soil moist.

STRELITZIA (Bird of Paradise Flower, Bird's Tongue Flower)
A handsome perennial growing from 3–5 ft high. The leaves are large and the flowers, shaped rather like a bird's head, are borne on stout spikes. *Time of flowering* Spring and early summer. *Propagation* (1) Division of the plants in spring. (2) Suckers in spring. (3) Seeds sown in spring in a temperature of 65–75°F and some bottom heat. *Position* Large pots in full sunlight. *Temperature* March to October 65–75°F, October to March 55–65°F. *General management* Pot fairly firmly in February or March. Plenty of water is needed while the plant is growing actively. Water sparingly in winter.

STREPTOCARPUS (Cape Primrose)
Large tubular flowers of many shades, pink, blue, violet, red, rosy-purple and white, are produced two or three together on stout stems. *Time of flowering* Summer. *Propagation* (1) Division of plants in March. (2) Leaf cuttings in summer. (3) Seeds sown in a temperature of 55–65°F in February, March or April. *Position* Pots shaded from bright sunlight. Young plants may be grown in shady cold frame during summer. *Temperature* April to October 55–65°F, October to April 40–50°F.

Feeding Feed once a week when the pots are comfortably full of roots. *General management* Old plants may be repotted in March. Seedlings should be potted on as they require it. Potting must always be done lightly. Water freely from April to October, but keep almost dry in the winter. Give plenty of ventilation during the summer.

TILLANDSIA (Old Man's Beard, Spanish Moss)
Perennials with rosettes of leaves and coloured bracts. *Time of flowering* Summer. *Propagation* Offsets in spring in a temperature of 75–85°F. *Position* Pots shaded from the sun. *Temperature* March to September 70–80°F, September to March 60–65°F. *General management* Repot in February or March. Water copiously in spring and summer, moderately at other times. Syringe once a day in spring and summer when a moist atmosphere is essential.

TRACHELIUM (Blue Throat-Wort)
Half-hardy perennial plants, growing about 2 ft high, with dense heads of tiny flowers. *Time of flowering* July and August. *Propagation* Seeds sown in spring or July in a temperature of 55–65°F. *Position* Pots in the sun. *Temperature* 40–45°F. *Feeding* Feed once a week when the pots are full of roots. *General management* Larger plants are obtained from the July sowing. The seedlings should be potted off singly when large enough and pinched occasionally to produce bushy growth, and the pots kept in a cold frame until October when they may be potted on into their flowering pots and moved into a cool house.

VRIESIA
Perennials very similar to Tillandsia. For propagation and cultivation see Tillandsia.

ZINGIBER (Ginger)
Perennial plants with large leaves and spikes of flowers. The roots are tuberous and produce the ginger of commerce. *Time of flowering* July. *Propagation* Division of the roots in February. *Position* Pots in shady part of house. *Temperature* March to October 75–85°F, October to March 55–65°F. *General management* Repot in February. Water copiously in spring and summer, but keep almost dry for the rest of the year.

13 Foliage plants under glass

This chapter deals mainly with herbaceous plants grown for the sake of their beautiful ornamental leaves. Full details for the correct culture of each plant are given. The plants appear in alphabetical order. Unless otherwise stated the John Innes or Alex Composts are used. The Seed Compost for seeds, and the No. 1 Potting Compost for all pottings.

A liquid manure specially for flowers is used for feeding the plants as and when necessary. Use according to the instructions on the bottle.

ACALYPHA (Three-sided Mercury, Copper Leaf)
Ornamental plants with orange-red, green and crimson leaves. *Propagation* Cuttings in February or March in a temperature of 80°F. *Position* Well-drained pots. *Temperature* March to September 70–80°F, September to March 60–65°F. *General management* Repot in February or March. Water freely in spring and summer, moderately in autumn and winter.

AGAVE (American Aloe, Century-Plant, Mexican Soap-plant)
Ornamental evergreen plants. Flowers are borne on spikes anything from 1 to 40 ft high only when the plants are at least ten years old. *Propagation* Offsets at any time. *Position* Pots or tubs which may be stood outside from June to September. *Temperature* Winter 50–55°F, Summer 55–65°F. *General management* Repot every five or six years. Water moderately from April to August, sparingly at other times.

ALOCASIA
Ornamental plants with short, thick stems and large arrow- or heart-shaped leaves, often variegated. *Propagation* Division of the rhizomes in March. *Position* Pots shaded from bright sunlight. *Temperature* March to September 70–80°F, September to March 60–65°F. *General management* Repot in March. The base of the plant should always be raised above the rim of the pot. Water freely in summer, moderately afterwards.

ANANAS (Pineapple)

(Often listed in catalogues as Ananassa.) The foliage is ornamental and evergreen. *Propagation* Suckers or crowns of fruit in spring in a temperature of 80°F. *Position* Pots in warm house fully exposed to sun. *Temperature* March to September 75–90°F, September to March 60–65°F. *Feeding* Feed freely when the plants are established in their fruiting pots. *General management* Water moderately in winter, freely in summer. A moist atmosphere is essential in spring and summer. Withhold water when the fruit begins to ripen. Plants should fruit when two years old.

ANTHERICUM

An ornamental plant with curving green leaves, striped and margined with white. *Propagation* (1) Division in March or April or October. (2) Seeds sown in cold frame in September or March. *Position* Pots in partial shade. *Temperature* March to October 55–65°F, October to March 45–50°F. *General management* Repot in March or April. Water freely from March to September, moderately at other times. The leaves should be syringed on bright days.

ARALIA (Angelica Tree)

Elegant ornamental plants with graceful growth and prettily divided leaves. *Propagation* (1) Root cuttings in April in a temperature of 80°F. (2) Cuttings of side shoots. (3) Grafting in spring on stocks of *A. guilfoylei* or *A. reticulata. Position* Pots shaded from strong sunlight. *Temperature* March to September 70–80°F, September to March 60–70°F. *General management* Repot in March. Water freely from March to October, moderately afterwards. Syringe the plants once a day during summer.

ARAUCARIA (Norfolk Island Pine)

Small conifers suitable for greenhouse decoration. *Propagation* (1) Cuttings of ends of young shoots in autumn. (2) Seeds sown from February to April in a temperature of 65°F. *Position* Well-drained pots or tubs in sunny house. *Temperature* March to October 55–65°F, October to March 45–55°F. *General management* Repot in March. Water freely during spring and summer, moderately at other seasons. The plants need plenty of room to develop and plenty of air in summer.

ASPARAGUS

Ornamental plants with fern-like foliage. *Propagation* (1) Division of roots in March. (2) Seeds sown in spring in a temperature of 65°F. *Position* Pots, tubs, beds or baskets. *Temperature* March to September 55–60°F, September to March 50–55°F. *Feeding* Established plants may be fed weekly. *General management* Repot old plants in March. Pot on young plants whenever they require it. Water and syringe freely during the summer, moderately at other seasons.

ASPIDISTRA (Parlour Palm)

Evergreen plants with large, wide leaves and peculiar, insignificant flowers just above the soil surface. *Propagation* Division of roots from March to September. *Position* Pots, shaded from strong sunlight. *Temperature* 50°F. *General management* The plants will thrive for years without repotting but when necessary this should be done in March. Water freely in summer, moderately in winter. If a variegated plant produces a green leaf, this must be cut out immediately, otherwise it may grow at the expense of the variegated ones.

BAMBUSA (Bamboo)

Graceful plants with grass-like foliage. *Propagation* (1) Division from March to May. (2) Cuttings of rhizomes in spring. (3) Seeds sown in spring. *Position* Large pots or tubs. *Temperature* 40–45°F. *General management* Repot in March. Water freely in spring and summer, moderately at other times.

BERTOLONIA

Trailing plants with ornamental foliage. *Propagation* Cuttings in spring in a temperature of 75°F. *Position* Well-drained pans shaded from bright sunlight. *Temperature* March to September 75–85°F, September to March 60–65°F. *General management* Repot February or March. Water freely in summer, sparingly in winter.

CALADIUM

Tuberous-rooted plants with ornamental, deciduous leaves, coloured green, white, crimson, red or rose. *Propagation* Division of the tubers in February or March. *Position* Well-drained pots shaded from bright sunlight. *Temperature* February to September 70–80°F, September to November 65–75°F, November to February 55–65°F. *General management* Pot up the tubers moderately firmly in February or March in pots just large enough to take them. Pot on in April or May. Water freely in summer, moderately in spring and autumn and keep quite dry in winter.

CAREX (Blue-Grass, Sedge)

A perennial with ornamental grass-like foliage. *Propagation* (1) Division of roots in March. (2) Seeds sown in March. *Position* Well-drained pots. *Temperature* 45–50°F. *General management* Repot in March. Plenty of water is needed during the growing season, less at other times.

CEROPEGIA

Trailing plants with ornamental leaves. *Propagation* Cuttings in spring in a temperature of 65°F. *Position* Baskets or pots in the sun. *Temperature* March to September 55–65°F, September to March 45–50°F. *General management* Repot in March. Water moderately in summer, sparingly in winter.

CODIAEUM (Croton or South Sea Laurel)

Shrubby, evergreen plants, the leaves beautifully marked with various colours. *Propagation* (1) Cuttings of shoots at any time in a temperature of 75°F. (2) Stem-rooting in March or April. *Position* Pots near the glass. *Temperature* March to October 70–85°F, October to March 55–65°F. *General management* Repot in March. Water freely in summer, moderately at other times.

COLEUS (Flame Nettle, Nettle Geranium)

Very ornamental plants with bright and variously coloured nettle-shaped leaves. *Propagation* (1) Cuttings of young shoots whenever available. (2) Grafting in spring. (3) Seeds sown in February in a temperature of 75°F. *Position* Pots in full sun. *Temperature* March to June 75–85°F, June to September 65–75°F, September to March 45–55°F. *Feeding* Feed the plants two or three times a week after the final potting. *General management* Pot fairly firmly in February or March. Young plants must be potted on as they require it and pinched back once to make them bushy and of a good shape. Water freely during the summer, moderately at other times.

COLOCASIA (West Indian Kale, Taro Root)

Tuberous-rooted plants 2–4 ft high, with ornamental leaves.

Propagation Division of the roots in February or March. *Position* Well-drained pots shaded from the sun. *Temperature* February to September 70–80°F, September to November 65–75°F, November to February 45–55°F. *General management* In February or March pot up the tubers moderately firmly in pots just large enough to hold them. Pot on in April or May. Water freely in summer, moderately in spring and autumn, but keep quite dry in winter.

CYPERUS (Umbrella Plant)

Ornamental plants with grass-like foliage and elegant flat flowering heads with greenish-brown flowers. *Propagation* (1) Division of roots in March and April. (2) Cuttings of heads of flowers, with small piece of stem attached. (3) Seeds sown in March or April in a temperature of 55–65°F. *Position* Pots in shady part of house. *Temperature* March to September 55–65°F, September to March 45–55°F. *Feeding* When the pots are full of roots, feed once a week. *General management* Repot February and March. Water moderately in winter, freely at other times. Syringe once a day.

DARLINGTONIA (Californian Pitcher-Plant)

Herbaceous insectivorous plant with ornamental foliage. The pitchers are borne on the summit of the leaves – they are hood-like, bright green and mottled, with white and pink. *Propagation* (1) Division of side-shoots at any time. (2) Seeds sown in mixture of fibrous peat, charcoal, sphagnum and sand in April or May. *Compost* Equal parts peat, chopped sphagnum, sharp silver sand and small pieces of limestone. *Position* Pots in shade. *Temperature* 55–60°F in summer, 45–50°F in winter. *General management* Repot in February or March. Water freely at all times and syringe daily in spring and summer.

DIEFFENBACHIA (Dumb Cane)

Plants with broad green leaves, variegated with white or yellow. *Propagation* Cuttings of stems 1–2 in. long in spring in a temperature of 75–85°F. *Position* Well-drained pots in moist atmosphere, shaded during the summer. *Temperature* February to September 65–85°F, September to February 55–65°F. *General management* Repot in February or March. Water freely in summer, moderately at other times. Syringe daily in summer.

DRACAENA (Dragon Plant, Dragon Tree)

Ornamental foliage plants requiring a stove temperature. The leaves are marked with various colours. *Propagation* (1) Cuttings of main stems or side shoots, 1 in. long and partially buried horizontally in the compost in March in a temperature of 85°F. (2) Root cuttings in March or April in a temperature of 75–80°F. (3) Stem rooting in March or April. (4) Offsets at any time. (5) Seeds sown 1 in. deep in March in a temperature of 85°F. *Compost* Two parts peat, one part loam and sand. *Position* Well-drained pots in light part of house, but shaded from very bright sunlight. *Temperature* March to September 75–85°F, September to March 65–75°F. *General management* Pot February and March. Water moderately in winter and freely in summer, and syringe the leaves during hot weather.

EULALIA (Zebra-striped Rush)

Ornamental grasses with light, elegant growth and narrow leaves. *Propagation* Division of plants in March or April. *Position* Pots shaded from bright sunlight. *Temperature* 40–50°F. *General management* Repot March or April. Water freely in summer, but in winter give only enough to keep the soil just moist.

FERNS

Foliage plants usually with graceful deeply cut leaves, green in colour or sometimes tinted with rather metallic shades. All need the same general treatment, though some will grow in the ordinary greenhouse, while others need a stove temperature. *Propagation* (1) Division of the plants in February or March, (2) Bulbils in the case of those species which form them. (3) Spores as soon as they are ripe in a temperature of 55–75°F. *Position* Pots or baskets, shaded from strong sunlight, or in borders beneath the staging. *Temperature* Hot-house species: March to September 65–75°F, September to March 55–60°F; Greenhouse species: March to September 50–60°F, September to March 40–50°F. *Feeding* Strong manures should never be given. Apply a weak solution occasionally to pot-bound plants. *General management* Repot moderately firmly in spring, when old fronds should be removed. Water freely in summer, moderately at other times, but soil must never be allowed to become too dry. Syringe the foliage in hot weather, and syringe between the pots in spring and summer.

FITTONIA
Evergreen trailing plants with ornamental foliage. *Propagation* (1) Division of plants in February or March. (2) Cuttings of firm shoots from February to April in a temperature of 75–85°F. *Position* Shallow pans, pots or beds in the shade. *Temperature* March to October 65–75°F, October to March 55–60°F. *General management* Pot or plant in spring. Water moderately in winter, freely at other times.

GYNURA
Perennial plants with purple-tinted ornamental foliage. *Propagation* Cuttings in spring. *Position* Pots in partial shade. *Temperature* March to October 70–80°F, October to March 55–65°F. *General management* Repot in March. Water freely in summer, moderately afterwards.

HELICONIA (False Plantain)
Plants with ornamental foliage, the stems are striped with black, green and yellow. *Propagation* Division of roots in February or March. *Position* Pots in shade. *Temperature* February to September 65–75°F, September to November 60–70°F, November to February 55–65°F. *General management* Repot February or March. Water freely in spring and summer, moderately in autumn, but keep dry in winter. Syringe daily in spring and summer.

ISOLEPIS (Club Rush)
Plant with grass-like drooping foliage, 6–12 in. long. *Propagation* (1) Division of plants in March. (2) Seeds sown in spring in a temperature of 60–65°F. *Position* Small pots, baskets or along the edge of the staging. *Temperature* March to October 55–65°F, October to March 45–55°F. *General management* Repot February or March. Water freely in spring and summer, moderately at other times.

LEEA
Ornamental shrubby plants with feather-shaped leaves, bronzy-green striped with white above and dark red below. *Propagation* Cuttings of side-shoots in spring in a temperature of 75–85°F. *Position* Well-drained pots in shade. *Temperature* March to September 65–75°F, September to March 55–65°F. *General management* Repot in February or March. Water freely in summer, moderately at other times. Syringe daily during the summer.

LEUCOPHYTA

Trailing shrubby plant with white cottony stems. *Propagation* Cuttings in August in a cold frame. *Position* Pots in the sun. *Temperature* 40–45°F. *General management* Repot in April. Water freely in summer, moderately at other times.

MARANTA (Arrowroot Plant)

Ornamental plants, the leaves are lance, heart or egg-shaped, round or oblong, and marked with various colours. *Propagation* Division of the plants in February or March. *Position* Well-drained pots in the shade. *Temperature* February to October 65–75°F, October to February 55–65°F. *Feeding* Feed plants occasionally during the summer. *General management* Repot each year in February or March. Water copiously in spring and summer, moderately in autumn and keep almost dry in winter. Syringe daily in summer.

MICONIA

Ornamental evergreen plants, leaves velvety, bronzy-green above, reddish-purple below. *Propagation* (1) Cuttings in spring in a temperature of 80–90°F. (2) Seeds sown in March or April in a temperature of 85°F. *Position* Pots in shade, atmosphere moist. *Temperature* March to September 75–85°F, September to March 60–70°F. *General management* Repot in February or March. Water moderately in winter, freely at other times. Syringe the plants in spring and summer.

MUSA

Perennials with ornamental large green leaves and edible fruits. The flowers are yellow, scarlet and green and are out from January to April. *Propagation* Suckers at any time in a temperature of 75–85°F. *Position* Pots, tubs or beds. *Temperature* March to October 70–80°F, October to March 60–70°F. *Feeding* Feed two or three times a week from March to October. *General management* Pot or plant from January to April. Water copiously from February to October, but sparingly in the winter. Syringe once a day in winter, twice a day in summer. A moist atmosphere is essential.

MYRSIPHYLLUM (Smilax)

Climbing plant with slender green shoots bearing oval leaves, small greenish-white flowers and dark purple berries. *Propagation* (1) Cuttings of young shoots in spring or summer. (2) Seeds sown in February in a temperature of 65°F. *Position* Pots, tubs, baskets or beds. *Temperature* March to September 60–65°F, September to March 50–55°F. *Feeding* Established plants should be fed occasionally. *General management* Pot or plant in March. Water and syringe freely during the summer, moderately at other times.

NEPENTHES (Pitcher Plant)
Ornamental shrubby plant. The leaves are oblong or lance-shaped, ending in a pitcher like appendage, coloured green and mottled with red, brown and crimson. *Propagation* (1) Cuttings of one-year-old shoots with bottom heat of 85°F at any time. Cuttings 6 in. in inverted flower pots, no soil but in very moist propagation frame. Keep closed. (2) Seeds sown on the surface of a mixture of fibrous peat and sphagnum moss in a temperature of 80–85°F. *Compost* Two parts fibrous peat, one part sphagnum moss. *Position* Baskets in shade. *Temperature* March to September 70–85°F, September to March 65–75°F. *General management* Plant in February or March. Water copiously in summer, moderately at other times. Syringe twice a day. A moist atmosphere is essential.

NIDULARIUM
Ornamental plants with leaves in rosettes, and green, red or crimson bracts. *Propagation* Offshoots from February to April in temperature of 85°F. *Position* Well-drained pots in light part of the house. *Temperature* March to September 70–80°F, September to March 60–65°F. *General management* Repot in February or March. Water moderately in winter, freely at other times.

PALMS
Decorative foliage plants, slow growing and useful when small for the ordinary sized house. *Propagation* Seeds sown any time in a temperature of 85°F. It is advisable to buy in young plants as the seeds require a high temperature for germination. *Position* Pots or tubs in partial shade. *Temperature* Summer 60–65°F, winter 45–55°F. *Feeding* Feed established plants once a week during the summer, and twice a week if roots are very restricted. *General management* Repot in early spring. There is no need to repot every year, the plants may remain in the same pots for several years provided they are top dressed each spring with a little fresh soil. Give plenty of water in summer

and keep the roots just moist in winter, sponge or syringe the foliage occasionally to remove dust, etc.

PANDANUS (Screw Pine)
Evergreen shrubby plants with ornamental foliage, leaves narrow and strap-shaped. *Propagation* Suckers from February to April. *Position* Pots in the sun. *Temperature* March to September 65–85°F, September to March 55–65°F. *General management* Repot from January to April. Water moderately in winter, freely at other times. Syringe twice a day in spring and summer. A moist atmosphere is essential.

PANICUM (Panick Grass)
A pretty trailing grass, the green leaves being striped with white and often with pink. *Propagation* Cuttings of young shoots in small pots three or four round one pot in a propagating frame in a temperature of 65–75°F any time. *Position* Small pots or baskets in sun or shade. *Temperature* March to September 60–75°F, September to March 55–65°F. *General management* Repot in March. Usually the cuttings are not potted up separately, but the three or four are potted on together. Water freely in summer, moderately in winter.

PELLONIA
Ornamental creeping plants, with roundish, oval or heart-shaped leaves, olive-green in colour with violet and white markings. *Propagation* (1) Division of plants in March or April. (2) Cuttings of shoots in spring in a temperature of 75–85°F. *Position* Shallow pans or beds beneath the staging. *Temperature* April to September 65–75°F, September to April 55–65°F. *General management* Pot or plant in March or April. Water moderately in winter, freely at other times.

PEPEROMIA (Pepper Elder)
Creeping perennial with ornamental foliage. *Propagation* Cuttings of shoots, or a single joint, with a leaf attached, in spring with bottom heat, and a temperature of 65–75°F. *Position* Shallow pans or beds, shaded from the sun. *Temperature* April to September 60–75°F, September to April 55–65°F. *General management* Pot or plant in March or April. Water moderately in winter, freely in summer. Syringe once a day in summer.

PHILODENDRON

Ornamental evergreen dwarf or climbing plants, leaves oblong, heart, egg or arrow shaped. *Propagation* Cuttings of stems in temperature of 75°F at any time. *Position* Dwarf kinds in pots, tall kinds in beds or borders. *Temperature* March to September 70–80°F, September to March 60–65°F. *General management* Pot or plant from January to April. Water freely and syringe daily.

PHYLLANTHUS

Ornamental plants. The leaves are small and oval, variegated with purple, white and yellow. *Propagation* Cuttings of firm shoots, 2–3 in. long in spring or summer in a temperature of 75°F. *Position* Well-drained pots in shade. *Temperature* March to September 70–80°F, September to March 60–65°F. *General management* Repot in February or March. Water freely in summer, moderately in winter, syringe twice a day in summer. Cut back into shape in January.

PHYLLOTAENIUM

Tuberous ornamental plants with leaves shaped like arrow heads. *Propagation* Division of roots in February or March. *Position* Well-drained pots in shade. *Temperature* February to September 70–80°F, September to November 65–75°F, November to February 55–65°F. *General management* Pot up the tubers moderately firmly in pots just large enough to take them in February or March. Pot on in April or May. Water freely in summer, moderately in spring and autumn and keep dry during the winter.

PILEA (Artillery or Pistol Plant, Stingless Nettle)

Dwarf foliage plants with small green leaves and insignificant flowers. *Propagation* (1) Division of plants in February or March. (2) Cuttings inserted singly in well-drained pots in temperature of 65–75°F from January to May. (3) Seeds sown in spring in temperature of 65–75°F. *Position* Small pots shaded from bright sunlight, or makes excellent baskets. *Temperature* March to September 70–80°F, September to March 45–55°F. *General management* Repot in February to April. Water freely in summer, moderately afterwards.

SANSEVIERA (Bowstring Hemp, Angola Hemp)

Plants with ornamental foliage. The flowers are insignificant, being white, green or yellowish. *Propagation* Division of plants from February to April. *Position* Pots in shade. *Temperature* March to September 65–75°F, September to March 55–65°F. *General management* Repot February to April. Water copiously in summer, moderately at other times. Syringe in summer.

SAXIFRAGA (Aaron's Beard, Mother of Thousands)
The shoots are long, slender and trailing, with tiny plantlets arising here and there all over the plant. *Propagation* (1) Division in spring. (2) Plantlets potted up singly in spring and summer. *Position* Small, well-drained pots or baskets in full sunlight. *Temperature* March to October 65–70°F, October to March 45–55°F. *General management* Repot in March or April. Careful watering is essential, and during the winter the soil should only be kept just moist.

SCHISMATOGLOTTIS
Dwarf ornamental plants, the leaves are oblong or heart-shaped, green and striped with silver grey. *Propagation* Division of plants in February or March. *Position* Well-drained pots in shade. *Temperature* March to September 75–80°F, September to March 60–65°F. *Feeding* Feed occasionally during the summer. *General management* Repot in February or March. Water copiously in summer, moderately afterwards. Syringe once a day during the summer. *General management* Repot in February or March. Water copiously in summer, moderately afterwards. Syringe once a day during the summer.

SELAGINELLA (Creeping Moss, Tree Club Moss)
Green mossy or fern-like, while others are dwarf, bushy or trailing. *Propagation* (1) Division. (2) Cuttings of shoots 3 in. long, any time except in winter in a temperature of 80°F. *Position* Pots or pans shaded from strong sunlight. *Temperature* March to September 55–65°F, September to March 40–50°F. *General management* Repot February or March. Several cuttings should be grown together in one pot. The roots must be kept moist all the year, but plants must be watered freely in summer and syringed daily.

ZEBRINA (closely akin to Tradescantia)
Plants with ornamental leaves. *Propagation* Cuttings in summer in a temperature of 75°F. *Position* Well-drained pots. *Temperature* March to September 65–75°F, September to March

45–55°F. *General management* Repot in March or April. Water freely in spring and summer, moderately at other times.

14 Shrubs and climbers

It is difficult in some cases to decide whether a plant is a shrub or a herbaceous flowering plant. The species mentioned in this chapter under shrubs are all plants with woody stems. Among the climbers, however, some are herbaceous and some are woody, and they are natural climbers, or trailing plants suitable for training up against a wall, rafter, etc.

All the species and varieties mentioned may be bought at a reasonable price, and they are not difficult to cultivate so long as they are given the conditions they require. The majority are included on account of their flowers, but some have, in addition, ornamental leaves or coloured attractive fruits.

(Composts and feeding as at the beginning of Chapter 13.)

Shrubs
ABELIA
Evergreen flowering shrub. *Time of flowering* Summer. *Propagation* (1) Cuttings of firm shoots in a cold frame in July. (2) Layers in March. *Position* Well-drained pots in the sun; outside during the summer; in cold frame from October to January. *Temperature* 40–45°F. *General management* Repot in October. Water freely when in full growth, moderately at other times, very little during the winter. *Pruning* Cut back straggly shoots after flowering.

ABUTILON
Shrubs and semi-climbers, useful for their fine foliage as well as their beautifully veined bell-shaped flowers. *Time of flowering* Spring and early summer. *Propagation* (1) Cuttings of side-shoots in spring or summer in a temperature of 65°F. (2) Seeds sown in March in a temperature of 70°F. *Position* Pots in the sun, or planted out in borders. *Temperature* March to September 55–65°F, September to March 50–55°F. *Feeding* Feed once a week when the pots are full of roots and the plants growing actively. *General management* Repot in March or top-dress plants in borders. Water freely in spring and summer, moderately in autumn and winter. *Pruning* In February thin shoots and trim into shape.

ACACIA (Wattle)

Trees and shrubs with yellow flowers and decorative pinnate leaves. *Time of flowering* Spring and early summer. *Propagation* (1) Heel cuttings of half-ripened shoots in June or July in a cold frame or inside a bell-jar. (2) Seeds sown in March in a temperature of 60°F. *Position* Pots or borders. Pots may be plunged outside after flowering until October. *Temperature* March to September 55–60°F, September to March 40–45°F. *General management* Repot firmly in summer, every three or four years. Water freely in spring and summer, moderately in winter. *Pruning* Immediately after flowering. Thin shoots and cut back straggling growths into shape.

ALOYSIA (Sweet-scented Verbena – usually sold now as Lippia)

A deciduous shrub with sweetly scented foliage and small lilac-pink flowers. *Time of flowering* August. *Propagation* Heel cuttings of young shoots 4 in. long in March, in a temperature of 65°F. *Position* Pots or borders. *Temperature* In winter, 45–50°F, at other times 50–55°F. *General management* Repot in spring when necessary. Water freely in summer, but little should be given in winter. May be grown as a bush or trained up a pillar. *Pruning* February. All the previous year's growths should be cut back to two or three buds.

AOTUS

Dwarf evergreen flowering shrubs, about 3 ft high, with slender shoots and graceful spikes of yellow and crimson flowers. *Time of flowering* May. *Propagation* Cuttings of half-ripened shoots in spring in a temperature of 55°F. *Position* Well-drained pots in the sun. *Temperature* March to September 55–60°F, September to March 45–50°F. *General management* Repot every two or three years in June or July. Plenty of water is necessary in summer and plants should be syringed daily. In winter the soil should be kept just moist. Ventilate freely during the summer. *Pruning* After flowering cut back shoots to keep the bushes shapely.

APHELANDRA

Evergreen flowering shrubs; the flowers are surrounded by beautifully coloured bracts. *Time of flowering* Autumn and winter. *Propagation* Cuttings of firm shoots in March or April in bottom heat. *Position* Pots in a warm house. *Temperature*

March to September 70–80°F, September to March 60–65°F. *General management* Repot in March. Water freely in summer, moderately in winter, but atmosphere should always be moist. *Pruning* Cut back shoots to within 1 in. of their base in February.

ARDISIA (Spear Flower)

Evergreen shrubby plant 3–4 ft high, with white flowers followed by red berries. *Time of flowering* June. *Propagation* (1) Cuttings of side-shoots in March in a temperature of 75°F, (2) Seeds sown in spring in a similar temperature. *Position* Pots in the sun. *Temperature* March to September 70–80°F, September to March 45–55°F. *General management* Repot in February or March. Water freely in summer, but give only a little in winter. *Pruning* Cut back straggly shoots closely in March.

Azalea indica, a lovely plant for the winter

AZALEA

Three types are commonly grown in pots under glass, hybrids and varieties of the so-called Indian Azaleas, with single or double flowers in all shades of red, pink and white; varieties of the Japanese *Azalea mollis*, a deciduous species, and obtainable in various shades of rose, orange, yellow and flame; and dwarf evergreen species. *Time of flowering* December to May. *Propagation* (1) Heel cuttings of half-ripened shoots in spring in a temperature of 65–75°F for Indian Azaleas. (2) Cuttings of half-ripened shoots in August in cold frame for *A. mollis*. (3) Grafting in spring for Indian Azaleas, and *A. mollis*. (4) Layering in spring after flowering for *A. mollis*. (5) Seeds sown when ripe in a temperature of 55–65°F for *A. mollis* and Indian Azaleas. *Compost* Lime must be omitted from the soil, add plenty of peat. *Position* Well-drained pots in the sun, October to June; in partial shade outside for the rest of the year. *Temperature* October to November 40–45°F, November to June 60–65°F. *Feeding* Feed once a week when the flower buds form. *General management* Repot firmly after flowering every two years. Water moderately October to March, freely at other times, but roots must never be allowed to become dry. Syringe once a day after flowering until the plants are put outside. *Pruning* Shorten back straggly growths after flowering and remove all seed pods.

BAUHINIA
Evergreen flowering shrubs. *Time of flowering* Summer. *Propagation* Cuttings in July in a temperature of 75°F. *Position* Pots in the sun. *Temperature* March to September 70–80°F, September to March 60–65°F. *General management* Repot firmly in March. Water freely in spring and summer, moderately at other times.

BORONIA (Australian Native Rose)
Dwarf evergreen shrubs with attractive fragrant flowers. *Time of flowering* April to June. *Propagation* Cuttings of firm young shoots, 2–3 in. long, from June to August, under a shaded bell-glass in a temperature of 50°F. *Position* Put pots outside in partial shade from June till August; in house for rest of year. *Temperature* March to September 50–60°F, September to March 45–50°F. *General management* Young plants must be stopped two or three times to promote bushy growth. Repot firmly when necessary directly after flowering. Water freely in summer, moderately at other times. *Pruning* Cut back shoots into shape after flowering.

BOUVARDIA
Dwarf evergreen shrubs with fragrant flowers. *Time of flowering* September to March. *Propagation* (1) Division in March. (2) Cuttings of young shoots 2–3 in. long in March in a temperature of 65°F. (3) Root cuttings 1 in. long in spring. *Position*

In cold frame from June to September, otherwise in warm house. *Temperature* February to September 55–75°F, September to February 45–55°F. *Feeding* Feed once a week from September to June. *General management* Repot at the end of March. Water moderately in spring, freely in summer, and only just keep moist in winter. Syringe the foliage once or twice a day in summer, and pinch back the shoots occasionally until the end of August. *Pruning* Towards the end of February shorten back the previous year's growths to within 1 in. of their base.

BRUNFELSIA
Evergreen flowering shrubs. *Time of flowering* Winter, spring or summer. *Propagation* Cuttings 2 to 3 in. long from February to August in a temperature of 60–70°F. *Position* Well-drained pots in warm house. *Temperature* March to October 60–70°F, October to March 45–55°F. *Feeding* Feed once a week in summer. *General management* Repot firmly immediately after flowering. Water moderately in winter, freely at other times. Syringe in spring and summer. *Pruning* Thin lightly after flowering. Pinch back young shoots when they are about 6 in. long.

BURCHELLIA (Bufflehorn – Wood)
Dwarf evergreen flowering shrub with scarlet flowers. *Time of flowering* March to May. *Propagation* Cuttings of young shoots from March to May in a temperature of 75°F. *Position* Well-drained pots in warm house. *Temperature* March to September 65–75°F, September to March 45–55°F. *General management* Repot in March. Water freely in summer, moderately at other times.

CALLISTEMON (Bottle Brush Tree)
Evergreen shrubs with leathery leaves and dense spikes of flowers. *Time of flowering* June. *Propagation* (1) Cuttings of ripe shoots, 3 in. long in summer under a bell-glass in a temperature of 55–65°F. (2) Seeds when available, but the seedlings take years before they reach the flowering stage. *Position* Pots or well-drained border in sunny well-ventilated house. *Temperature* March to September 55–65°F, September to March 40–50°F. *General management* Repot every two or three years or plant in March or April. Water freely in summer, moderately afterwards, but they should never be allowed to

become dry at the roots. Syringe the foliage during hot weather. *Pruning* After flowering cut back lightly.

CAMELLIA (Tea-Plant)

Large evergreen flowering shrubs, not suitable for small houses. *Time of flowering* Early spring. *Propagation* (1) Cuttings of firm shoots in July. (2) Layering in September. (3) Grafting in March. (4) Seeds sown in March in temperature of 75°F. *Position* Large pots or tubs or in borders. Pot plants may be stood outside from June to September. *Temperature* March to September 55–65°F, September to March 50–55°F. *Feeding* Feed once a week from August to March. *General management* Repot every three years in March or April, or top dress those plants in borders. Water freely in summer, moderately in winter, and syringe daily during the summer. *Pruning* March. Very little is necessary. Straggling shoots only should be shortened.

CASSIA (Senna Plant)

An evergreen, growing 6–10 ft high, producing bunches of yellow, pea-like flowers. *Time of flowering* Summer and autumn. *Propagation* Cuttings of half-ripe shoots in spring or early summer in temperature of 80°F. *Position* Well-drained pots which may be stood outside from June to September. *Temperature* March to September 55–65°F, September to March 50–55°F. *General management* Repot in March. Water freely in summer, but very little is needed in winter. *Pruning* In December or January cut back straggling shoots to within 2 in. of base.

CENTRADENIA

Dwarf evergreen flowering shrub. *Time of flowering* July. *Propagation* Cuttings of side-shoots 2–3 in. long in February and March in a temperature of 85°F. *Position* Pots in the sun. *Temperature* March to September 65–75°F, September to March 45–55°F. *General management* Repot in February. Water freely in spring and summer, moderately at other times.

CHOISYA (Mexican Orange-Flower)

Hardy evergreen flowering shrub with white flowers, suitable for culture in pots. *Time of flowering* Summer. *Propagation* Cuttings of shoots, 3 in. long from March to June in a temperature of 55–65°F. *Position* Pots in cool house from November to May, outside for the remainder of the year. *Temperature* 45–50°F. *General management* Repot in September or October. Water moderately in autumn and winter, freely at other times. *Pruning* Shorten back straggling shoots after flowering.

CHORIZEMA

Evergreen flowering shrubs with red and yellow flowers. *Time of flowering* April. *Propagation* (1) Cuttings in summer in a temperature of 65°F. (2) Seeds sown in March in a temperature of 65–70°F. *Position* Pots or well-drained borders. Pot plants may be put outside from July to September. *Temperature* March to September 55–65°F, September to March 45–50°F. *General management* Repot firmly in March or June. Water freely in spring and summer, moderately at other times. *Pruning* Cut back straggling shoots lightly after flowering.

CITRUS (Orange)

Evergreen shrubs with white fragrant flowers and large orange fruits. *Time of flowering* May or July. *Propagation* (1) Cuttings in July. (2) Layering in October. (3) Grafting in March. (4) Budding in August. (5) Seeds sown ½ in. deep in March in a temperature of 55°F. *Position* Well-drained pots, tubs or beds. Trees in pots or tubs may be stood in a sheltered position outside from June to September. *Temperature* February to September 55–65°F, September to February 45–50°F. *Feeding* Feed once a week from May to October. *General management* Repot when necessary from February to April. Water freely in spring and summer, moderately at other times. Syringe once a day in summer. *Pruning* Cut back into shape in March.

COLUMNEA

Evergreen trailing shrubs with scarlet and yellow flowers. *Time of flowering* June. *Propagation* Cuttings of firm shoots 3in. long in February in temperature of 85°F. *Compost* Equal parts of peat, sphagnum moss and charcoal. *Position* Hanging baskets. *Temperature* March to September 70–80°F, September to March 60–65°F. *Feeding* Give liquid manure at least once a week during the summer. *General management* Plant in March. Water freely in summer, moderately at other times.

CORONILLA (Crown Vetch, Scorpion Senna)

An evergreen shrub with numerous fragrant, yellow pea-like flowers. *Time of flowering* Spring and summer. *Propagation*

(1) Cuttings of young shoots in April in a temperature of 55°F or in August in a cold frame. (2) Seeds sown in March in a temperature of 75°F. *Position* Pots may be put outside from June to September. *Temperature* March to September 55–65°F, September to March 40–45°F. *General management* Repot in March. Plenty of water is needed in summer, but little in winter. *Pruning* Bushes need clipping back into shape in March.

CORREA (Australian Fuchsia)

Pretty evergreen shrubs, 3–6 ft high. *Time of flowering* Spring and summer. *Propagation* (1) Cuttings in April in a temperature of 65–75°F. (2) Side grafting in heat in March, on to *C. alba* or *Eriostemon buxifolius. Position* Well-drained pots in light well-ventilated house. Pots may be put outside during August and September if weather is fine. *Temperature* March to September 55–65°F, September to March 40–45°F. *General management* Repot when necessary in July when new growth begins. Careful watering is necessary at all times, very little being needed in the winter, syringe freely in bright weather. *Pruning* Directly after flowering, cut back all shoots which have flowered, to maintain a well-shaped bush. (Note: In some catalogues the spelling is Corroea.)

CROSSANDRA

Dwarf evergreen shrub with orange-scarlet flowers. *Time of flowering* March. *Propagation* Cuttings of shoots 2–3 in. long at any time in a temperature of 85°F. *Position* Pots in warm, moist house. *Temperature* March to October 75–85°F, October to March 55–65°F. *General management* Repot in March. Water moderately in winter, freely at other times.

CYTISUS (Broom)

One species is often grown in pots. It makes a compact bush and freely produces bunches of small, fragrant, yellow laburnum-like flowers. *Time of flowering* Spring and early summer. *Propagation* (1) Heel cuttings in March or August of young shoots 2–3 in. long in a temperature of 75–80°F. (2) Seeds sown in March in a temperature of 65–70°F. Seedlings do not always come true to type. *Position* Pots which may be stood outside in sun from July to October. *Temperature* October to February 45–50°F, February to May 50–55°F, May to June 55–60°F. *Feeding* Once a week when the plants are in flower. *General management* Repot in May or June. Young plants should be stopped two or three times to produce bushy growth. Water freely from March to May and from June to November, but moderately at other times. Syringe freely in hot weather. *Pruning* After flowering cut back shoots to within 2 in. of their base.

DAPHNE
Small evergreen shrubs with fragrant flowers. *Time of flowering* March. *Propagation* (1) Cuttings of well-ripened side-shoots in October and November in a temperature of 50–55°F. (2) Layers in March or April. (3) Grafting in spring on to seedling plants of *D. laureola* or *D. potica. Position* Airy house from September to June; outside for remainder of year. *Temperature* March to September 55–65°F, September to March 40–50°F. *General management* Repot in March or April after flowering. Very little water is needed in winter, but should be given freely in summer; syringe plants on hot days. Always use lime-free soil. *Pruning* Cut back young shoots into shape in June.

DATURA (Angel's Trumpet)
Large evergreens, with enormous trumpet-shaped flowers, only suitable for large houses. *Time of flowering* Summer and early autumn. *Propagation* Cuttings of shoots 6 in. long in spring or autumn in a temperature of 65–75°F. *Position* Large pots or tubs, or planted in the borders of a sunny house. Pot plants may be stood outside in sun from June to September. *Temperature* March to September 55–65°F, September to March 45–55°F. *Feeding* Feed occasionally while the plants are in flower. *General management* Repot, top dress or plant in March. Water freely in the summer, but very little in the winter. Syringe the plant freely during the growing period.

DESFONTAINEA
Hardy evergreen shrub with dark shiny green oval leaves with spiny edges, and scarlet and yellow flowers. Suitable for greenhouse culture. *Time of flowering* August. *Propagation* Cuttings in spring in a temperature of 55–65°F. *Position* Well-drained pots, tubs or borders. *Temperature* 40–45°F. *General management* Repot or plant in March or April. Water moderately in winter, freely at other times.

DEUTZIA (Japanese Snow-Flower)

Although hardy shrubs, at least one species is suitable for growing in pots. The leaves are deciduous and the flowers small and white and produced in large numbers. *Time of flowering* Spring. *Propagation* Cuttings of young shoots 3 in. long in spring. *Position* In pots in house February to May; outside May to November, and in a cold frame from November until February. *Temperature* 55–65°F. *Feeding* Feed occasionally. *General management* Pot up in October or November. Water moderately in spring, freely in summer, but give little at other times. Although not necessary, it is advisable after flowering to plant the bushes outside for a year, when they may again be lifted for pot work. *Pruning* After flowering, cut away as much as possible of the old wood which has borne flowers.

DIOSMA (African Steel-Bush)

Dwarf evergreen shrubs with fragrant foliage. *Time of flowering* Spring. *Propagation* Cuttings in spring in a temperature of 60°F. *Position* Pots in cool house. *Temperature* March to September 50–55°F, September to March 40–45°F. *General management* Repot in May or June. Water moderately in summer, but little should be given in winter. *Pruning* Pinch back vigorous shoots in summer to promote bushy growth.

EPACRIS (Australian Heath, Tasmanian Heath)

Small evergreen shrubs with heath-like flowers. *Time of flowering* March to June. *Propagation* (1) Cuttings of young shoots in May or June or August. (2) Seeds sown as soon as they are ripe in a temperature of 55°F. *Compost* 3 parts fibrous peat, 1 part silver sand. *Position* In a light, well-ventilated house from September to July; outside in a sunny place for the rest of the year. *Temperature* September to March 45–50°F, March to July 55–60°F. *General management* Repot firmly in April, May or June. Water moderately at all times. Syringe plants daily from March to July. *Pruning* Directly after flowering cut back shoots of erect kinds to within 1 in. of their base. Pendulous kinds are just cut back into shape.

ERICA (Heath)

Shrubby evergreen plants 1–2½ ft high. They may be divided into two groups, the hard-wooded kinds which are rather difficult to grow, and the soft-wooded types which are seen in the markets as pot plants. *Time of flowering* December to

August. *Propagation* Cuttings of shoots 1 in. long in spring in a temperature of 60–70°F. *Compost* 3 parts of good fibrous peat well broken up and 1 part sharp silver sand, and, if possible, 1 part 'pulled' or rough peat. *Position* Light, airy house October to July, outside in the sun July to October. *Temperature* October to March 40–45°F, March to July 45–55°F. *Feeding* Feed occasionally. *General management* Repot firmly autumn and winter-flowering kinds in March, and summer-flowering sorts in September. Water carefully, always seeing that the soil is sufficiently moist. It is important to use rain water. *Pruning* Immediately after flowering. Slow growers only require strong shoots pinching back into shape. Free growing kinds should have strongest growths cut back to within 1 or 2 in. of their base and the weakest shoots tipped.

ERIOSTEMON

Small evergreen shrubs. *Time of flowering* May and June. *Propagation* (1) Cuttings in March or August, of half-ripe shoots 2 in. long, in a temperature of 60°F. (2) Grafting on to stocks of *Correa alba* in March. *Position* Well-drained pots in light airy house. Outside in the sun from July to September. *Temperature* April to September 50–60°F, September to April 40–45°F. *General management* Repot firmly in March. Water carefully at all times. Syringe daily in summer. *Pruning* Cut back straggling growths in February.

ERYTHRINA (Coral Tree)

Deciduous shrub bearing bunches of pea-shaped, scarlet flowers. *Time of flowering* June to August. *Propagation* Heel cuttings of young shoots in spring in a temperature of 75°F. *Position* Pots in warm house. *Temperature* March to September 55–65°F, September to March 45–60°F. *Feeding* Feed frequently when plants are well-rooted. *General management* Repot in March. Water freely from April to September, but keep almost dry for the rest of the year. Store pots on their sides during winter. *Pruning* Cut back shoots close to their base in November.

EUCALYPTUS (Australian Gum)

Most species develop into large timber trees, but there are several suitable for pot culture, in the young stages. The leaves are evergreen, and are covered with a greyish bloom and are pleasantly scented. *Propagation* (1) Cuttings of side-shoots in gentle bottom heat. (2) Seeds sown in early spring in a temperature of 65°F. *Position* Pots in warm house. *Temperature* 45–50°F in winter, 55–60°F in summer. *General management* The best plan is to raise young plants from seed each year, otherwise repot in March or April. Water moderately in winter, freely in summer. *Pruning* None is required.

EUGENIA (Fruiting Myrtle)
Evergreen shrub with narrow leaves, white flowers and globular, fragrant fruits. *Time of flowering* Summer. *Propagation* Cuttings of firm shoots in summer in a temperature of 55–75°F. *Position* Pots in warm house. *Temperature* March to October 55–65°F, October to March 40–50°F. *General management* Repot in February or March. Water freely in summer, moderately at other times. Syringe during the summer. *Pruning* Cut back straggling shoots in March.

EUPHORBIA
Flowering shrubs, some with ornamental leaves and bracts. *Time of flowering* Summer to winter. *Propagation* Cuttings of young shoots 3 in. long from May to July in a temperature of 70°F. *Position* Pots in the sun. *Temperature* January to May 50–55°F, May to September 65–75°F, September to January 55–65°F. *General management* Repot in March or June. Water moderately from September to January; keep almost dry from January to May and water freely for the rest of the year. *Pruning* Cut back shoots of *E. fulgens* to within 1 in. of their base in June.

EURYA
A dwarf evergreen shrub. *Propagation* Cuttings of young shoots in spring in a temperature of 60–65°F. *Position* Pots in cool house. *Temperature* 45–50°F. *General management* Repot in March or April. Water freely in summer, moderately at other times. *Pruning* Little required.

FABIANA (False Heath)
Dwarf evergreen shrubs with heath-like foliage and white flowers. *Time of flowering* Spring. *Propagation* Cuttings of firm young shoots in April or August in cold frame. *Position* Pots in cool house. *Temperature* 40–45°F. *General management* Repot in summer. Keep the roots fairly moist all the year round. *Pruning* Cut back shoots lightly after flowering.

FATSIA (Fig Leaf Palm, Japanese Aralia)
Evergreen shrub with large, leathery leaves. *Propagation* (1)
Cuttings of stems 2 in. long in spring. (2) Cuttings of roots in
March or April in a temperature of 80°F. (3) Variegated kinds
are grafted on to common species in March or April in
temperature of 75°F. (4) Stem rooting in spring for tall plants.
(5) Seeds sown in a temperature of 65°F. *Position* Well-drained
pots in cool house. *Temperature* April to September 55–65°F,
September to April 40–50°F. *General management* Repot in
spring. Water freely in summer, moderately at other times.

FICUS
Evergreen shrubs with decorative foliage. *Propagation* (1)
Cuttings of shoots in spring and summer in a temperature of
75°F. (2) 'Eyes' i.e. small pieces of stem about 1 in. long
containing a bud, with a leaf attached, in a temperature of
75°F. (3) Stem rooting in spring. *Position* In pots or beds,
shaded from strong sunlight. *Temperature* February to October
65–75°F, October to February 55–60°F. *General management* Pot
or plant from February to April. Water freely in summer,
moderately at other times. Syringe daily in hot weather.

FUCHSIA (Lady's Ear Drops)
Attractive flowering shrubby plants. *Time of flowering* Summer.
Propagation (1) Cuttings of young shoots from January to
March in a temperature of 70–80°F or from April to June or
September, in cool house. (2) Seeds sown in March or April
in a temperature of 55°F. *Position* Pots in house shaded from
strong sunlight from March to July: outside in ths sun from
July to October; in a cool, dry place for the rest of the year.
Temperature October to February 40–45°F, February to Octo-
ber 55–65°F. *Feeding* Feed once a week when the plants are
well established. *General management* Repot old plants in
February or March; young plants as they need it. Pinch young
shoots frequently to make plants bushy. Water moderately
March to May, freely May to October and very little at other
times. Syringe plants daily from February till May. *Pruning*
Cut back fairly hard in February.

GARDENIA
Evergreen shrubs very much prized for their fragrant white
flowers. *Time of flowering* Spring and summer. *Propagation*
Cuttings of firm young side-shoots 2–3 in. long from January

Ficus pumila, the rubber plant

to April in a temperature of 70°F. *Position* Well-drained pots or beds shaded from strong sunshine. *Temperature* March to September 65–85°F, September to March 55–65°F. *Feeding* Feed occasionally when plants are in flower. *General management* Repot or plant in February or March. Water freely in summer, moderately in winter. Syringe daily in spring and summer except when in bloom. One- or two-year-old plants produce the best flowers. *Pruning* Cut back into shape in February.

GLONERIA (Psychotria)
Dwarf evergreen shrub with snow-white flowers. *Time of*

flowering Summer. *Propagation* Cuttings in spring in a temperature of 75–85°F. *Position* Pots in shade while growing; in light part of house during resting period. *Temperature* March to September 75–85°F, September to March 55–65°F. *Feeding* Feed once a week when the plants are in flower. *General management* Repot in February or March. Water freely in spring and summer, moderately at other times. Syringe twice a day during spring and summer. *Pruning* Cut back into shape in February.

GREVILLEA (Silk-Bark Oak)
Evergreen shrubs with flowers and ornamental foliage. *Time of flowering* Summer. *Propagation* (1) Heel cuttings of young shoots 3 in. long from March to May in a temperature of 75–80°F. (2) Seeds sown ¼ in. deep in March in a temperature of 65–70°F. The seeds are large and flat and should be placed in the pots point downwards or sideways, not flat. *Position* Well-drained pots in airy house. *Temperature* March to October 55–65°F, October to March 45–55°F. *General management* Repot firmly in March or April. Water freely in summer, moderately at other times. *Pruning* None for *G. robusta*. Other species need cutting back occasionally to keep them bushy and of a good shape.

HABROTHAMNUS or CESTRUM (Bastard Jasmine)
Evergreen or semi-evergreen flowering shrubs. *Time of flowering* Spring and summer. *Propagation* Heel cuttings of side-shoots 3–4 in. long from July to September in a temperature of 65–75°F. *Position* Pots or beds. *Temperature* March to September 55–60°F, September to March 40–50°F. *General management* Repot in March. Water moderately in winter, freely at other times. *Pruning* Cut back into shape in February.

HELIOTROPIUM (Heliotrope, Cherry Pie)
Shrubs with fragrant flowers. *Time of flowering* Spring to winter. *Propagation* (1) Cuttings of young shoots 2–3 in. long in March, April, August or September in a temperature of 65–75°F. (2) Seeds sown in March in a temperature of 65–75°F. *Position* Pots or beds. Makes quite good standard. *Temperature* February to October 60–70°F, October to February 50–55°F. *Feeding* Feed once a week when in flower. *General management* Pot or plant February to May. Water freely in summer, moderately at other times. *Pruning* Cut back old plants closely in February.

Young plants should be pinched back to produce bushy growth.

HIBISCUS

Evergreen shrub with large rose-like flowers. *Time of flowering* Summer. *Propagation* (1) Cuttings of firm shoots in spring or summer in a temperature of 75°F. (2) Grafting in March. (3) Seeds sown in March in a temperature of 75°F. *Position* Well-drained pots or beds. *Temperature* March to October 65–75°F, October to March 55–65°F. *General management* Repot or plant in February or March. Water copiously in spring and summer, moderately at other times. *Pruning* Cut back into shape in February.

HYDRANGEA

Deciduous shrubby plants with large heads of flowers. *Time of flowering* Spring and summer. *Propagation* Cuttings of young shoots in March or April in a temperature of 50–60°F or of firm shoots 2–3 in. long in August in a cold frame. *Position* Pots in cool house. *Temperature* 55–65°F. *Feeding* Feed once a week when plants are growing vigorously. *General management* Repot in February or March. Give plenty of water in summer, but very little in winter. Pink varieties, especially rich pink shades, may be tinged blue by treating the soil or the water. The best substance appears to be aluminium sulphate, crystals of which are added to the soil when potting the plants; $\frac{1}{4}$ oz to each 5-in. pot or $\frac{1}{2}$ oz to each 6-in. pot. If added in water, $\frac{3}{4}$ oz is sufficient for one gallon, and must first be dissolved in a little hot water. To be successful, the soil must be free from lime. White varieties will not respond to the treatment. *Pruning* In August or September remove weak shoots and cut back those which have flowered.

IXORA (West Indian Jasmine)

Evergreen, compact shrubs with trusses of fragrant flowers. *Time of flowering* Summer. *Propagation* Cuttings of firm young shoots 2–3 in. long from March to May, in a temperature of 75–85°F. *Position* Well-drained pots in the shade during growing season, in light part of house during resting period. *Temperature* March to September 75–85°F, September to March 55–65°F. *Feeding* Feed once or twice a week when plants are in flower. *General management* Repot in February or March. Water freely in spring and summer, moderately at other seasons. Syringe twice a day in spring and summer. *Pruning* Cut back into shape in February.

LAGERSTROEMIA (Indian Lilac, Queen's Flower, Cape Myrtle)

Evergreen flowering shrubs. *Time of flowering* Summer. *Propagation* Cuttings of firm shoots in March, April, August or September in a temperature of 65–70°F. *Position* Well-drained pots in light house. *Temperature* March to October 60–70°F, October to March 45–55°F. *Feeding* Feed occasionally when pots are filled with roots. *General management* Repot February or March. Water freely in summer, sparingly in winter. Syringe daily during summer. *Pruning* Cut back fairly hard in November or December.

LASIANDRA (Brazilian Spider-Flower)

Evergreen shrub with purple flowers. *Time of flowering* Summer. *Propagation* Cuttings of firm side-shoots 3 in. long from February to September in a temperature of 70–80°F. *Position* Well-drained pots, tubs or beds. *Temperature* March to September 60–70°F, September to March 45–55°F. *Feeding* Feed once a week from May to September. *General management* Pot or plant in February or March. Water freely in summer, moderately at other times. *Pruning* Cut back into shape in February.

LEONOTIS (Lion's Ear)

Dwarf evergreen shrub with orange-scarlet flowers. *Time of flowering* Summer. *Propagation* Cuttings of shoots in March or April in a temperature of 55–65°F. *Position* Well-drained pots in light, well-ventilated house from September to June; outside in the sun for the rest of the year. *Temperature* September to April 40–50°F, April to June 55–65°F. *General management* Repot in March or April. Water moderately in spring and summer, sparingly at other times. *Pruning* Cut back into shape after flowering.

LUCULIA

Evergreen flowering shrubs with leathery foliage. *Time of flowering* Autumn. *Propagation* (1) Cuttings of young shoots in June or July in a temperature of 70–80°F. (2) Seeds sown from February to April in a temperature of 60–70°F. Seedlings flower when 3–5 years old. *Position* Large, well-drained pots or beds. *Temperature* April to September 60–70°F, September to December 55–65°F, December to April 45–55°F. *General management* Pot or plant between February and April. Water freely from April to November but the roots should be kept almost dry for the rest of the year. Syringe twice a day in summer. *Pruning* After flowering cut back young shoots to 2 or 3 in.

MEDINILLA
Dwarf evergreen flowering shrubs. *Time of flowering* Spring. *Propagation* Cuttings of firm young side-shoots, 3–4 in. long in spring or summer in a temperature of 85°F. *Position* Pots in sunny, moist part of the house from February to September; in a light fairly dry part at other seasons. *Temperature* February to September 75–85°F, September to November 70–80°F, November to February 60–65°F. *Feeding* Feed once a week when plants start to flower. *General management* Repot in February. Water freely in spring and summer, moderately at other times. Syringe twice a day in spring and summer. *Pruning* Cut back straggly shoots into shape in January or February.

MUSSAENDA
Evergreen shrubs with yellow flowers. *Time of flowering* Autumn and winter. *Propagation* Cuttings of young shoots from May to July in a temperature of 70–80°F. *Position* Well-drained pots in a light part of the house. *Temperature* February to October 65–85°F, October to February 55–65°F. *General management* Repot from February to April. Water freely from April to September; moderately from February to April and September to November, and keep almost dry during the remaining months. Syringe once a day in spring and summer. *Pruning* Cut back and thin lightly after flowering.

MYRTUS (Myrtle)
Evergreen shrub with ornamental green fragrant foliage, and white sweetly scented flowers followed by oblong or round, purplish-black berries which are fragrant and edible. *Time of flowering* May to July. *Propagation* (1) Cuttings of young shoots 2 in. long in spring or summer in a temperature of 65–75°F. (2) Heel cuttings of firm shoots 2–3 in. long in autumn in a temperature of 60°F. *Position* Well-drained pots, tubs or borders. Pots may be stood outside in sunny place from June

to September. *Temperature* March to September 55–65°F,
September to March 45–50°F. *Feeding* Feed once a week
during the summer. *General management* Pot or plant in
February or March. Water copiously in summer, moderately
afterwards. Syringe once a day during the summer. *Pruning*
Cut back into shape in February.

NERIUM (Oleander, Rose Bay)

Evergreen shrubs with fragrant flowers. *Time of flowering*
Summer. *Propagation* Cuttings of firm young shoots 3–6 in. long
in spring or summer in a temperature of 60–70°F. *Position* Pots,
tubs or well-drained beds in a sunny part of the house. Plants
in pots or tubs may be stood outside from June till September.
Temperature September to March 45–55°F, March to June
55–65°F. *Feeding* Feed once or twice a week during the
summer. *General management* Repot or plant in February or
March. Water copiously in spring and summer, moderately in
autumn, and keep almost dry in winter. Syringe twice a day
from March to June. *Pruning* Immediately after flowering, or
in October, shorten back shoots of previous year's growth to
within 3–4 in. of their base. Remove young shoots that are
produced from the bases of the flower trusses as soon as they
appear.

OCHNA

Evergreen shrubs with yellow flowers, followed by black and
crimson globular fruits. *Time of flowering* Spring. *Propagation*
Cuttings of firm shoots 2–3 in. long in summer in a temperature of 65–75°F. *Position* Well-drained pots in the sun. *Temperature* March to September 70–75°F, September to March
45–55°F. *General management* Repot in February or March.
Water freely in spring and summer, moderately at other times.
Syringe once a day in spring and summer. *Pruning* Cut back
into shape in February.

OLEA (Olive)

Evergreen shrub with white fragrant flowers. *Time of flowering*
Summer. *Propagation* (1) Cuttings in summer. (2) Seeds sown
in spring or autumn. *Position* September to May in pots in a
cool greenhouse, outside for the rest of year. *Temperature*
September to May 40–50°F. *General management* Repot in
March. Water freely in summer, moderately at other times.
Syringe once a day in summer. *Pruning* Thin out when
necessary.

PAVETTA

Dwarf shrub with white flowers and ornamental leaves. *Time of flowering* June to August. *Propagation* Cuttings of firm young shoots 2–3 in. long from March to May in a temperature of 75–85°F. *Position* Well-drained pots in shade while growing, in light part of house when plants are resting. *Temperature* March to September 60–70°F, September to March 45–55°F. *Feeding* Feed once or twice a week when plants are in flower. *General management* Repot in February or March. Water freely in spring and summer, moderately at other times. Syringe twice a day in spring and summer. *Pruning* Cut back into shape in February.

PHYLLAGATHIS

Shrub 1–2 ft high with pink flowers, large glossy green and tinged with metallic blue and purple, and red beneath. *Time of flowering* July. *Propagation* Leaf cuttings in a temperature of 85°F and bottom heat. *Position* Well-drained pots. *Temperature* March to September 75–85°F, September to March 60–65°F. *General management* Repot in March. Water copiously during the growing season, moderately at other times. A moist atmosphere is essential during the summer.

PIMELEA (Rice Flower)

Dwarf evergreen shrubs with pink flowers freely produced. *Time of flowering* May. *Propagation* (1) Cuttings of young shoots 2 in. long in March or April in a temperature of 55–65°F. (2) Seeds sown from February to May in a similar temperature. *Position* Well-drained pots in a light well-ventilated house. *Temperature* March to September 55–65°F, September to March 40–50°F. *General management* Repot firmly as soon as new growth starts in the spring. Water freely in summer, moderately at other times. Syringe during summer. *Pruning* Cut back into shape immediately after flowering, removing all the dead flower heads. Stop young shoots occasionally to induce bushy growth.

POINSETTIA

Shrubby plants with insignificant flowers, but the bracts are bright red or white. The leaves are green or variegated with creamy-white. *Time of flowering* Autumn. *Propagation* Cuttings of young shoots 2–3 in. long in May with bottom heat of 85°F. *Position* In pots in a cold frame shaded from the mid-day sun

A Poinsettia makes a good plant for Christmas time

from July to September, afterwards in warm house. *Tempera-*
ture September to April 55–60°F, April to July 65–75°F.
Feeding Feed twice a week from October till the bracts are fully
developed. *General management* Repot in spring. Water and
syringe freely while growing, after flowering keep quite dry.
Pruning Cut back shoots to 2 or 3 buds in April.

POLYGALA (Milk Wort)
Evergreen shrubby plant 4–6 ft high, with rich purple pea-
shaped flowers. *Time of flowering* April till June. *Propagation*
Cuttings of young shoots 3 in. long in spring in a temperature
of 50°F. *Position* Well-drained pots in a well-ventilated house.

Shaded from mid-day sun. Place in a cold frame from July to September. *Temperature* March to September 55–65°F, September to March 40–50°F. *General management* Repot in February or March. Water freely in summer, moderately at other times. Syringe twice a day in bright weather except when the plants are in bloom. *Pruning* Cut back straggly shoots into shape in February.

PUNICA (Pomegranate)

Fairly large deciduous trees with roundish golden-red fruits. Suitable for small houses in the seedling stage. *Time of flowering* June to September. *Propagation* Double-flowered kinds. (1) Cuttings of firm shoots 6–8 in. long. (2) Layering shoots in October or November. (3) Grafting on single-flowered species in March. (4) Seeds sown in spring in a temperature of 55–65°F. *Position* In well-drained pots, tubs or borders with shoots trained against a wall. *Temperature* 40–45°F. *General management* Pot or plant from October to February. Water freely in summer, moderately in autumn and spring, none in winter. *Pruning* Cut back weak shoots only in early spring.

RHODODENDRON

Greenhouse kinds are not so popular as they were at one time, but well-grown plants make a fine display. *Time of flowering* Careful selection will give bloom for the greater part of the year. *Compost* Two parts turfy loam, one part peat, one part silver sand. *Position* Well-drained pots or tubs outside in the sun from June to September, in warm house for the rest of the year. *Temperature* March to June 55–65°F, September to March 45–55°F. *Feeding* Feed occasionally when the buds show. *General management* Repot firmly every three or four years in April or May, or directly after flowering. Water freely in summer, moderately at other times, using rain water if possible, since the plants will not tolerate water containing lime. *Pruning* Cut back straggly growths only, and remove seed pods after flowering.

RONDELETIA

Evergreen shrub, 4–6 ft high, with fragrant tubular orange-red flowers with a yellow throat. *Time of flowering* Summer. *Propagation* Cuttings of firm shoots in spring or summer, in a temperature of 75–85°F. *Position* Well-drained pots in light part of house, but shaded from bright sunshine. *Temperature*

March to September 70–80°F, September to March 55–60°F. *General management* Repot in February or March. Water freely in spring and summer, moderately at other times. Syringe once a day in spring and summer. *Pruning* Cut back lightly after flowering.

RUSSELLIA (Coral-Blow)

Dwarf evergreen shrubs with red two-lipped tubular flowers, suitable for hanging baskets. *Time of flowering* July. *Propagation* (1) Cuttings in spring in a temperature of 75°F. (2) Layering at any time. *Position* Baskets or pots in light part of house. *Temperature* March to September 65–75°F, September to March 45–55°F. *Feeding* Feed once a week when in flower. *General management* Repot in February or March. Water freely in summer, moderately at other times. Syringe twice a day in summer except when in flower. *Pruning* Thin lightly in February.

SANCHEZIA

Ornamental shrub, 3–4 ft high, with fairly large tubular yellow and red flowers. *Time of flowering* March to October. *Propagation* Cuttings of young shoots from March to July under a bell-glass. *Position* Shady part of house in spring and summer, light part for the rest of the year. *Temperature* March to September 75–85°F, September to March 55–65°F. *Feeding* Feed occasionally during the summer. *General management* Repot in March. Water freely in spring and summer, moderately at other times. Syringe twice a day in spring and summer.

SPARMANNIA (African Hemp)

An evergreen shrub up to 10 ft high, but plants 3–4 ft high flower well. The flowers are white and the numerous stamens are sensitive when young and move when touched. *Time of flowering* Summer. *Propagation* Cuttings in spring and summer in a temperature of 55–65°F. *Position* Pots in a light, well-ventilated house from September to June, outside in the sun for the rest of the year. *Temperature* March to September 55–65°F, September to March 40–50°F. *Feeding* Feed once a week from April to September. *General management* Repot in February or March. Water freely in spring and summer, moderately at other times. *Pruning* Cut back fairly close in December or January.

STROBILANTHES (Cone Head)

Dwarf evergreen shrub with long, iridescent leaves, purple beneath and violet flowers in spikes. *Time of flowering* Autumn. *Propagation* Cuttings of fairly firm shoots, 2–3 in. long, from February to April in a temperature of 80°F. *Position* Well-drained pots in a light part of the house. *Temperature* March to September 75–85°F, September to March 60–65°F. *Feeding* Feed twice a week when plants are in flower. *General management* Repot in March or April. Water freely in summer, moderately at other times. Syringe frequently during the growing season. It is important to maintain a moist atmosphere. *Pruning* Cut back shoots closely in February.

SWAINSONIA (Darling River Pea)

Evergreen shrubs growing 3 or 4 ft high, with sprays of pea-like flowers useful for cutting. *Time of flowering* Summer. *Propagation* (1) Cuttings of young shoots 2–3 in. long from April to July. (2) Seeds sown in March or April in a temperature of 55–65°F after being soaked for about an hour in tepid water. *Position* Well-drained pots, tubs or borders in the sun; outside from June to September. *Temperature* September to March 35–45°F, March to June 55–65°F. *Feeding* Feed occasionally in summer. *General management* Repot or top-dress in February or March. Water freely in spring and summer, moderately at other times. Syringe once a day in summer except when the plants are in flower. *Pruning* Cut back into shape about a fortnight before repotting.

TABERNAEMONTANA (Adam's Apple, East Indian Rose Bay)

Evergreen shrubs about 6 ft high with yellowish-white flowers. *Time of flowering* June. *Propagation* Cuttings of ripe shoots, 2–3 in. long in February in a temperature of 65–75°F. *Position* Well-drained pots in a light part of the house. *Temperature* March to September 70–80°F, September to March 60–65°F. *General management* Repot from February to April. Water freely in spring and summer, moderately at other times. Syringe once a day from March until the flowers appear. *Pruning* Cut back straggling shoots lightly immediately after flowering.

THYRSACANTHUS (Thyrse Flower often called Odontonema)

Evergreen shrub, 3–6 ft high, with drooping spikes of tubular red flowers. *Time of flowering* Winter. *Propagation* Cuttings of young shoots from March to July in a temperature of 75°F. *Position* Well-drained pots in light part of house from September to June; outside in a sunny frame for the rest of the year. *Temperature* September to March 45–55°F, March to June 65–75°F. *Feeding* Feed twice a week when the plants are in flower. *General management* Repot in March or April. Water freely in spring and summer, moderately at other times. *Pruning* Cut back shoots to within 1 in. of their base after flowering. Pinch back the young shoots occasionally during the summer to produce bushy growth.

TREVESIA
Stove shrubs with yellowish-white flowers. *Propagation* Cuttings of half-ripened shoots under a bell-glass in a temperature of 80°F. *Position* Large, well-drained pots, shaded from strong sunlight. *Temperature* March to September 70–80°F, September to March 60–65°F. *General management* Repot in February or March. Water freely during the growing season, moderately at other times. A moist atmosphere is essential during the summer.

TRISTANIA
Evergreen shrub with small yellow flowers. Not suitable for small houses. *Time of flowering* July to September. *Propagation* Cuttings of half-ripe shoots in July or August, under a bell-glass with gentle bottom heat. *Position* Well-drained pots or borders. *Temperature* March to September 55–65°F, September to March 45–55°F. *General management* Repot in March or April. Water freely during the growing season, moderately at other times.

VERONICA
Several of the shrubby species are useful for growing in pots in the greenhouse. They are evergreen with flowers of various shades of pink, red, mauve or purple. *Time of flowering* Early autumn. *Propagation* (1) Cuttings of half-ripened shoots in August in a cold frame. (2) *V. hulkeana* by cuttings of young shoots in spring or August. *Position* Pots in the sun. Outside from May to September. *Temperature* 45–55°F. *Feeding* Feed once a week during the growing season. *General management* Repot in September or March. Water freely in spring and summer, moderately at other times. It is advisable to raise

some young plants each year as old ones require large pots and are not really satisfactory if the roots are restricted. *Pruning* Cut back shoots after flowering.

Climbers

ALLAMANDA
Evergreen climbing plant usually with large yellow funnel-shaped flowers. *Time of flowering* Summer. *Propagation* Cuttings of shoots 3 in. long of the previous year's growth in January in a temperature of 80°F. *Position* Pots, tubs or borders with the shoots trained close to the roof. *Temperature* March to September 70–80°F, September to March 60–65°F. *General management* Repot in February. Water in spring and summer, moderately at other times. *Pruning* Cut back shoots closely in January.

ARISTOLOCHIA (Birth-wort)
Strong-growing climbing plants with heart-shaped leaves and bent, oddly shaped flowers. *Time of flowering* Summer. *Propagation* (1) Cuttings in February in a temperature of 75°F. (2) Seeds sown in March in a similar temperature. *Position* Pots or borders with the shoots trained close to the roof. *Temperature* March to September 70–80°F, September to March 60–65°F. *General management* Repot in March. Water freely in summer, but give very little in winter. *Pruning* Cut back straggling shoots only.

BOUGAINVILLEA
Deciduous climbers with small, greenish inconspicuous flowers, but with brightly coloured bracts. Suitable for training up walls or pillars or over wire frames. *Time of flowering* Summer and autumn. *Propagation* Heel cuttings of young shoots 3 in. long from March to May in a temperature of 70–80°F. *Position* Well-drained pots or borders. *Temperature* February to May 55–60°F. May to September 65–75°F, September to February 50–55°F. *Feeding* Feed well-rooted plants occasionally during the growing season. *General management* Pot, plant or top-dress in February. Water copiously in spring and summer, moderately in autumn, none in winter. *Pruning* Cut back shoots of the previous year's growth to within 1 in. of their base in February.

CAMPSIS formerly called BIGNONIA (Cross-Vine, Trumpet-Flower)
Deciduous strong-growing climbers with fairly large flowers. *Time of flowering* Spring, summer and autumn. *Propagation* (1) Cuttings of young shoots 3 in. long in April in a temperature of 65–70°F. (2) Layering young shoots at the end of the summer. *Position* Well-drained pots or borders in the sun. *Temperature* March to October 55–65°F, October to March 45–55°F. *General management* Pot or plant firmly in February or March. Water freely in spring and summer, but very little at other times. Syringe once a day in hot, dry weather. *Pruning* Cut away weak growths as they appear, and shorten the remaining shoots in January.

CLEMATIS
One species is suitable for culture in the greenhouse. The flowers are white. *Time of flowering* April. *Propagation* (1) Cuttings in spring in a temperature of 75°F. (2) Seeds sown in spring in heat. *Position* Pots or well-drained beds. *Temperature* March to September 55–65°F, September to March 45–55°F. *General management* Pot or plant in spring. Water freely in summer moderately at other times. Syringe once a day in summer. *Pruning* Cut out weak growths and shorten strong ones a little in February.

CLERODENDRON (Glory-Tree)
Stove climber with heart-shaped leaves and fairly large flowers. *Time of flowering* Summer. *Propagation* (1) Cuttings of shoots 3 in. long from January to March in a temperature of 70–75°F. (2) Seeds sown in March in a temperature of 75°F. *Position* Pots or beds. *Temperature* February to October 65–85°F, October to February 55–60°F. *General management* Pot or plant in February. Water freely in spring and summer, moderately in autumn and keep dry in winter. *Pruning* Cut back shoots after flowering to within 2 or 3 in. of their base.

CLIANTHUS (Parrot's Bill, Sturt's Desert Pea)
Climbers with richly coloured pea-shaped flowers. *Time of flowering* April and May. *Propagation* (1) Cuttings of shoots in March or April in a temperature of 75–85°F. (2) Seeds sown in March in a temperature of 75°F. *Position* Well-drained pots or beds, with the shoots trained up walls or pillars. *Temperature* March to October 55–65°F, October to March 45–50°F.

General management Pot or plant in March. The plants dislike frequent disturbance. Water freely in spring and summer, moderately at other times. Syringe once a day in summer. *Pruning* Shorten young shoots to within 2 in. of their base.

COBEA (Cup and Saucer Plant, Mexican Ivy)
An easily-grown climber with large bell-shaped purplish flowers. *Time of flowering* Summer. *Propagation* Seeds sown in March in a temperature of 75°F. *Position* Pots or beds. *Temperature* March to September 60–70°F, September to March 45–55°F. *General management* Pot or plant in March. Water freely in summer, moderately at other times. *Pruning* Cut hard back in February.

DIPLADENIA
Stove evergreen climbers with large funnel-shaped flowers. *Time of flowering* Summer. *Propagation* Cuttings of young side-shoots 3 in. long from February to April in a temperature of 80°F. *Position* Well-drained pots with the shoots trained near the roof. *Temperature* February to October 65–75°F, October to February 55–60°F. *General management* Pot in February or March. Water freely in summer, moderately in spring and sparingly for the rest of the year. *Pruning* Cut back shoots which have flowered in October.

GLORIOSA (Malabar Glory Lily, Mozambique Lily)
Deciduous, tuberous-rooted climbers. The leaves are prolonged into tendrils and the red and yellow flowers are lily-like. *Time of flowering* Summer. *Propagation* (1) Offsets at potting time. (2) Seeds sown $\frac{1}{4}$ in. deep in February or March in a temperature of 75°F. *Position* Well-drained pots with the shoots trained near the roof. *Temperature* February to September 70–85°F, September to February 55–65°F. *General management* Pot up the tubers 2 in. deep in February. Water moderately until plants are growing strongly, then freely. After flowering, water sparingly and then keep dry until potting time.

HIBBERTIA
Slender evergreen climbers with small, heath-like leaves and fairly large yellow flowers. *Time of flowering* Summer. *Propagation* Cuttings of fairly firm shoots 3 in. long from April to August, under a bell-glass in a temperature of 55–65°F. *Position* Pots, tubs or beds with the shoots tied up the rafters.

Temperature March to October 55–75°F, October to March 45–55°F. *General management* Pot or plant in February or March. Water freely in spring and summer, moderately at other times. *Pruning* Cut back straggling shoots in February.

HOYA (Honey-plant, Wax Flower)

Evergreen climbers, with thick leaves and wheel-shaped flowers in clusters. *Time of flowering* Summer. *Propagation* (1) Cuttings of shoots of the previous year's growth from March to May in a temperature of 75–85°F. (2) Layering shoots in spring or summer. *Position* Well-drained pots, beds or hanging baskets with shoots trained up against the walls, but fully exposed to the light. *Temperature* Stove species: March to October 65–75°F, October to March 55–65°F; Greenhouse species: March to September 55–65°F, September to March 45–55°F. *General management* Pot or plant in February or March. Water freely in spring and summer, moderately at other times. *Pruning* Cut back into shape in February.

IPOMAEA (American Bell-bind, Moon Creeper, Morning Glory)

Climbers with Convolvulus-like flowers, useful for clothing pillars. *Time of flowering* Summer or winter. *Propagation* (1) Cuttings of side-shoots from March to August in a temperature of 75–85°F. (2) Seeds sown in March or April in a temperature of 60°F. *Position* Pots, beds or borders with the shoots trained near the roof. *Temperature* March to September 65–75°F, September to March 55–65°F. *General management* Pot or plant from February to April. Water freely in spring and summer, moderately at other times. *Pruning* Cut back straggly growth in February.

JASMINUM (Jasmine, Jessamine)

The species suitable for greenhouse cultivation are almost evergreen and more or less climbing in habit, so are easily trained up against a wall. *Time of flowering* Autumn and winter. *Propagation* (1) Cuttings of firm shoots from March to September under a bell-glass in a temperature of 65–75°F. (2) Heel cuttings of young shoots in spring under a bell-glass in a temperature of 60°F. *Position* Well-drained pots or borders with the shoots trained up near the roof. *Temperature* Stove species: March to September 65–75°F, September to March 55–65°F; Greenhouse species: March to September 55–65°F,

September to March 45–55°F. *General management* Pot or plant in February or March. Water freely in spring and summer, moderately at other times. Syringe once a day in spring and summer. *Pruning* Cut back lightly in February.

LAPAGERIA

These evergreens are among the most beautiful of greenhouse climbers. *Time of flowering* Summer. *Propagation* (1) Layering strong shoots in spring or autumn. (2) Seeds sown in March or April in a temperature of 55–65°F. *Position* Well-drained pots, tubs or beds in the shade. *Temperature* March to October 55–65°F, October to March 40–50°F. *General management* Pot or plant in February or March. Water freely in spring and summer, moderately at other times. Syringe once a day from March until the flowers develop. Ventilate freely in spring and summer. *Pruning* Cut out dead or weak shoots in March.

MANDEVILLA (Chile Jasmine)

Only one species is grown. This is a deciduous climber bearing numbers of large, white, sweetly scented flowers. *Time of flowering* Summer. *Propagation* (1) Cuttings of firm side-shoots 2–3 in. long, in April or May in a temperature of 70–85°F. (2) Seeds sown from February to April in a temperature of 65–75°F. *Position* Well-drained beds where the shoots can be trained up near the roof to receive plenty of light and air. *Temperature* February to September 55–65°F, September to December 45–55°F, December to February 40–50°F. *General management* Plant in February. Water freely in spring and summer, moderately in autumn and keep dry in winter. Syringe twice a day from February to July. *Pruning* Cut back weak shoots closely during the winter.

MANETTIA

Evergreen twining climber with small tubular scarlet and orange flowers. *Time of flowering* March to December. *Propagation* (1) Cuttings of young shoots 2–3 in. long in summer in a temperature of 65–75°F. (2) Seeds sown in February or March in a temperature of 55–65°F. *Position* Well-drained pots or beds with the shoots trained up near the roof. *Temperature* February to October 55–65°F, October to February 45–55°F. *General management* Pot or plant in February or March. Water freely in spring and summer, moderately at other times. Syringe once a day from March to September. *Pruning* Cut back lightly after flowering.

MITRARIA (Mitre Flower, Scarlet Mitre-pod)

There is only one species, a half-hardy evergreen climber with bright scarlet flowers. *Time of flowering* May to August. *Propagation* (1) Cuttings of shoots from April to September in a cold frame or under a bell-glass. (2) Division of the roots in April. *Position* Well-drained pots in the shade. *Temperature* 45–50°F. *General management* Pot in September for October or March. Water freely in spring and summer, moderately in autumn, sparingly in winter. *Pruning* Cut back the shoots slightly in winter.

MONSTERA

Evergreen climber with yellow flowers, ornamental large, thick, dark green leaves perforated with large holes and cylindrical edible fruits. These are fragrant and pineapple flavoured and ripe in the autumn. *Time of flowering* Summer. *Propagation* Cuttings of stems at any time in a temperature of 70–80°F. *Position* Well-drained border against a damp wall. *Temperature* March to September 65–75°F, September to March 55–65°F. *General management* Plant February to April. Water freely in spring and summer, moderately at other times. Syringe twice a day in spring and summer, once a day at other times.

PASSIFLORA (Passion Flower)

Vigorous climbers suitable for covering walls, rafters and pillars. They have long spiral tendrils and sometimes edible fruits. *Time of flowering* Summer. *Propagation* (1) Cuttings of young shoots 4–6 in. long from April to September in a temperature of 65°F. (2) Seeds sown $\frac{1}{4}$ in. deep at any time in a temperature of 65–75°F. *Position* Well-drained pots, tubs or beds with the shoots trained near the glass in the sun. *Temperature* Stove species: March to October 65–75°F, October to March 55–65°F; Greenhouse species: March to October 55–65°F, October to March 45–50°F. *Feeding* Feed plants occasionally when in flower. *General management* Repot or plant in February or March. Water copiously in spring and summer, moderately at other times. Syringe twice a day in spring and summer. *Pruning* To prevent overcrowding remove some of the weak shoots as they appear. In February cut out weak shoots and shorten back strong ones.

PETREA (Purple Wreath)

A deciduous climber, with rough, leathery leaves and blue flowers in long racemes. *Time of flowering* Summer. *Propagation* Cuttings of firm young shoots in spring and summer under a bell-glass in a temperature of 65–75°F. *Position* Well-drained pots or beds with the shoots trained up the rafters in the shade. *Temperature* March to September 65–75°F, September to March 45–55°F. *General management* Pot or plant in February or March. Water freely in spring and summer, moderately at other times. Syringe once a day in spring and summer. *Pruning* Cut back lightly in February.

PLUMBAGO (Cape Leadwort)

A shrubby climber, usually deciduous so that it does not shade other plants in the winter. *Time of flowering* Summer or winter. *Propagation* (1) Heel cuttings of side-shoots 2–3 in. long from February to August in a temperature of 60–70°F. (2) Seeds sown in February or March in a temperature of 65–75°F. *Position* Pots or borders with the shoots trained near the glass in a light part of the house, but shaded from strong sunlight. *Temperature* Stove species: March to October 75–85°F, October to March 55–65°F; Greenhouse species: March to October 55–65°F, October to March 45–55°F. *Feeding* Feed twice a week during the flowering period. *General management* Pot or plant from February to April. Water freely in spring and summer, moderately at other times. Syringe once a day until the flowers start to appear. *Pruning* Cut back stove species moderately in January. Cut back shoots of greenhouse species to within 9 in. of their base immediately after flowering.

RHODOCHITON

Only one species which is suitable for the greenhouse but not recommended for small houses. It is a climber with reddish-purple flowers. *Time of flowering* Summer. *Propagation* (1) Cuttings of shoots from March to August under a bell-glass in a temperature of 45°F. (2) Seeds sown in March in a temperature of 50–60°F. *Position* Well-drained pots, boxes or beds with the shoots trained up near the glass, but shaded from bright sun. *Temperature* March to September 55–65°F, September to March 45–55°F. *Feeding* Feed once a week during the flowering period. *General management* Pot or plant from March to May. Water freely in spring and summer, moderately at other times. The main shoots should be tied up, allowing the

slender side-growths to hang down, thus giving a graceful
effect. *Pruning* Thin out and shorten shoots lightly in February.

RHYNCHOSPERMUM (Chinese Jasmine)

An easily grown evergreen climber, growing 10–15 ft high
with small trusses of very fragrant white flowers. *Time of
flowering* Summer. *Propagation* Cuttings of firm young shoots
2–3 in. long in spring or summer, under a bell-glass in a
temperature of 65–75°F. *Position* Well-drained pots or borders
with the shoots trained up the walls or pillars but shaded from
the sun. *Temperature* 45–50°F. *General management* Pot or plant
in April or May. Water freely in spring and summer, moderately at other times. Syringe once a day in summer. *Pruning*
Thin and cut back into shape after flowering.

SOLANUM

Climbers with decorative flowers. *Time of flowering* Summer.
Propagation Cuttings of young shoots in late spring and early
summer in gentle bottom heat. *Position* Pots, tubs or beds with
the shoots trained up the rafters. *Temperature* March to
September 65–75°F, September to March 45–55°F. *General
management* Pot or plant firmly in March. Water freely in
spring and summer, moderately at other times. *Pruning* Cut
away weak growths and shorten others in February.

SOLLYA (Australian Bluebell Creeper)

Evergreen twiners which flower freely, producing deep blue
flowers. *Time of flowering* Spring and summer. *Propagation*
Cuttings of young shoots in spring and summer under a bell-
glass in a temperature 65–75°F. *Position* Well drained pots or
beds with the shoots trained up against the walls or rafters.
Temperature March to September 55–65°F, September to
March 40–50°F. *General management* Pot or plant in February
or March. Water freely in spring and summer, moderately at
other times. Syringe daily in summer.

STEPHANOTIS (Clustered Wax-flower,
Madagascar Jasmine)

Stove evergreen twining shrubs with white fragrant flowers.
Time of flowering Spring and summer. *Propagation* Cuttings of
shoots of the previous year's growth in spring under a bell-
glass in a temperature of 65–75°F. *Position* Well-drained pots,
tubs or beds with the shoots trained up the rafters, but shaded

from the sun. *Temperature* March to October 70–85°F, October to March 45–55°F. *Feeding* Feed once a week between May and September. *General management* Pot or plant in February or March. Water copiously in spring and summer, moderately at other times. Syringe daily in spring and summer, except when the plants are in bloom. *Pruning* Cut back straggling shoots moderately closely and thin out weak shoots in January or February.

STIGMAPHYLLON (Golden Vine)
A stove evergreen climber with clusters of showy yellow flowers. *Time of flowering* June to September. *Propagation* Cuttings of firm shoots in spring or summer, under a bell-glass in a temperature of 65–75°F. *Position* Well-drained pots with the shoots trained up the roof. *Temperature* March to September 70–85°F, September to March 55–65°F. *General management* Pot in February or March. Water freely in spring and summer, moderately at other times. Syringe once a day during the summer. *Pruning* Cut away the weak growths and shorten strong shoots moderately in January.

STREPTOSOLEN
A free-flowering evergreen climber with clusters of bright orange flowers. Excellent for clothing a back wall. *Time of flowering* April to July. *Propagation* Cuttings of young shoots in spring or summer in a temperature of 55–65°F. *Position* Well-drained pots close to the glass, but shaded from strong sunlight. *Temperature* March to October 60–70°F, October to March 45–55°F. *Feeding* Feed occasionally during the summer. *General management* Pot February to April. Water freely in spring and summer, moderately at other times. Syringe once a day in spring until the flowers appear. Give plenty of ventilation in spring and summer. *Pruning* Cut shoots back fairly closely after flowering.

TACSONIA (Blood-red Passion Flower)
Attractive plants closely related to the Passion flower. They are vigorous evergreen climbers so are most suitable for fairly large greenhouses. *Time of flowering* Summer and autumn. *Propagation* As for Passiflora.

THUNBERGIA (Clock Vine)
Evergreen climbers with funnel-shaped flowers. *Time of*

flowering Spring and summer. *Propagation* (1) Cuttings of firm young shoots 2–3 in. long from February to June in a temperature of 75–85°F. (2) Seeds sown from January to May in a similar temperature. *Position* Well-drained pots or beds with shoots trained up the roof. *Temperature* February to October 65–75°F, October to February 55–65°F. *Feeding* Feed occasionally from May to September. *General management* Pot in February or March. Water freely in spring and summer, moderately in autumn and keep almost dry during the winter. Syringe once a day in spring and summer. *Pruning* Cut back lightly in February.

15 Cacti and succulents

Cacti and succulents attract people because of their quaintness. They are not difficult to grow, and many of them flower annually. There is no need to fear them (as so many people do) because of possible poisoning, for they are no more dangerous than roses. Some of the Opuntias have minute bristles, which may set up a skin irritation if handled carelessly, but this is soon cured by the use of thick Calendula ointment.

Succulents often appeal in preference to cacti, for they have no spines. They will also grow in a less sunny position; their foliage is varied and beautiful, and they have fat, juicy green leaves.

There are at least 2,000 different kinds of cacti, and they fall into three big groups. Within these groups there are 124 genera in all. The generic name of the plant may be said to be its surname, and the species name or specific name its Christian name.

Cacti flowers may be yellow, scarlet, pink, magenta, orange or white. The white ones usually flower at night, and are generally sweetly scented. Some flowers last for several days, and others only for a few hours.

Fruits often follow the flowers; some look like scarlet berries, others are almost hidden until they release their seeds, some may be like walnuts and others like small pears. Some of the berries of the Mammillaria taste like the strawberry.

SIMPLE NOTES ON CULTIVATION

More cacti and succulents are killed by being coddled than by being neglected. It must be remembered that in their natural conditions they have to struggle for existence. All they ask for is plenty of fresh air, light and sunshine, and a certain amount of moisture.

WATERING CACTI

It is very difficult to be dictatorial about water. Normally it shouldn't be necessary to water from the end of September to

A flowering cactus

the beginning of March. The actual time of starting will depend upon weather conditions and on the climate. In Cornwall and Devon, for instance, it may be necessary to start watering at the end of February, while in the Manchester district or round Huddersfield, watering may be delayed until the middle of April. The first watering should certainly be done by standing the pot in water at the same temperature as the house nearly up to the rim, and only removing it when the soil at the top shows the moisture. When soaked in this way they shouldn't require any more water for a month. They can then be dipped again as before.

During the summer when the sun is really hot, they may need dipping once a week. About the middle of August the dipping should only be done once a fortnight so that the plants will get hardened off for the winter.

The soil should always be allowed to dry out before the plants are watered again.

WATERING SUCCULENTS
Succulents do require a little water in the winter, and many of them flower then. They should not be soaked, but the pots may be stood in a tray containing water to the depth of $\frac{1}{4}$ in.

for an hour or so, and only when the weather is mild and bright. It is inadvisable to water succulents in December and January.

The succulents, however, should not be watered during their resting periods, and these differ according to the species. The Lithops need a rest from Christmas until the end of April, and the Conophyta from the beginning of May to the beginning of August. Mesembryanthemums will go for a couple of months without being watered at almost any time of the year.

TYPE OF WATER

Rainwater should be used whenever possible. The water should be at the same temperature as the house or frame.

SYRINGING

Cacti may be syringed over during the months of June and July, in the evening just as the sun is going to rest. Early in May they can be given a good forceful spraying with water at the same temperature as the house in order to remove the winter dust, and to help start them into growth. The succulents with delicate foliage should not be treated in this way.

IN THE HOUSE — WATERING

Cacti in the house usually need more water than cacti in the greenhouse. The atmosphere in a room is considerably dryer. This means that dipping may have to take place once a fortnight, even throughout the winter. Care should be taken to see that the water is at the same temperature as the pot.

COMPOSTS AND POTTING

Cacti should be grown in a very open compost; one that has been found satisfactory consists of one third good heavy soil, fairly free of organic matter, one third coarse sand and one third broken brick or burnt clay. To this mixture may be added a small quantity of granulated charcoal, and an equally small measure of pounded-up clean egg-shell.

The Phyllocacti can do with a slightly richer compost, and so a little peat can be added or a small portion of spent mushroom bed. The Echinopses and Cerei may also have a little fibrous peat, because they are used to moister conditions.

Though cacti grow quite well in small pots, they always do better if they are given sufficient root run. Before potting, the pots should be washed thoroughly, and new pots should be soaked well. The diameter of the pot at the top should be not less than the diameter of the cactus including the length of the spines. Over the drainage hole should be placed a small piece of perforated zinc made convex. On top of this artificial crock should be placed some burnt clay or charcoal, and such drainage material should extend a third of the way up the pot.

When potting, the roots of the plants should be spread out and the neck should be covered. Deep planting is advisable, on the whole, so as to encourage the formation of roots higher up. A half-inch space should be left on the top of the soil to allow for watering. The compost should not be firm but the pot should be knocked two or three times on the potting bench to assist it in settling.

When potting, it is advisable to use leather gloves, and if the plants are large, sheets of newspaper may be wrapped around them to assist in easy handling.

Every two years the plants may need repotting into slightly larger pots, and this should be done early in the spring. The old soil should be shaken from the roots, and any that are damaged may be cut back with the sharp blade of a knife. A similar compost as advised above should be used fairly dry, and no water need be given until the beginning of the growing season. It is possible to pot back into the same pot after it has been washed.

The year the plant is not being potted on, the surface soil in the pot should be scratched over with a pointed stick, and a little powdered charcoal worked in.

VENTILATION

Keep the ventilators open every day except when it is wet or foggy. During the summer they may be kept open day and night, but during the winter they should be closed in the afternoon so as to keep out the frost.

SUN AND LIGHT

Everything possible should be done to keep the glass of the greenhouse clean. In and around towns the glass will need scrubbing with warm soapy water every autumn and spring, both outside and in. A good deal of friction has to be used if the greasy soot stains are to disappear. Rain will certainly not achieve this object. If the gutters feed the rainwater tank these should be disconnected during the washing down process.

In some years, and in the case of seedlings, a little shading may be necessary from the midday sun during a very hot spell.

HEATING

The house may be heated by warm water pipes, by electricity or by gas stoves. (See Chapter 3.)

The minimum temperature at night time should be about 38–40°F and in the day 45°F. During the day the temperature may be allowed to rise to 60 or 70°F with the sun heat.

Should the greenhouse not be heated, the plants should be covered with brown paper when there is any prospect of a frost at night or during the day. If it should freeze during the night and the plants be covered with brown paper, and the sun come out brightly the following morning, the paper should be left over the plants until the temperature of the house has risen somewhat.

Brown paper is sometimes used as an additional protection where the heating apparatus is on the small side.

PROPAGATION

Most cacti can be raised from seeds sown at any time during the year if heat is available. Beginners will find it best to sow during the months of May, June and July. Sowing should be done inside a propagating case in the greenhouse. The box may be kept warm by placing it over the pipes, or if heated electrically by controlling the extra heat in the propagating case by a thermostat. The temperature in the case should be 75°F.

The compost for seed sowing should consist of equal parts of horticultural peat moss and coarse silver sand passed through a fine sieve. A small quantity of powdered charcoal may be added. This compost should be placed into clean pots or pans which are at least 4 in. deep. The lowest inch should be filled with broken crocks or broken bricks to allow perfect drainage. The seeds should be sown $\frac{1}{2}$ in. apart, and be lightly covered with equal parts of sand and charcoal dust. The pots or pans should then be placed in shallow trays filled with water, these being placed inside the propagating box.

If the temperature and the moisture in the propagating case are kept constant the seeds should germinate in three or four days. Give some shade until this happens by means of a sheet of brown paper. As the plants grow more air and light should be given, and when the seedlings are fit to handle they may be potted up into baby thumb pots in a compost consisting of equal parts of good soil, horticultural sedge peat, sand and charcoal (in small pieces). A little garden lime may be dusted on. It should then be possible to grow the plants in a temperature of 65°F.

Some cacti can be propagated by means of cuttings. Side branches may be cut off during the growing season, and provided the cut is a clean one the cutting left to dry for a day or so, it may be struck in a mixture of equal parts of fine horticultural peat and pure silver sand. The pot in which the cutting is placed should contain plenty of drainage material at the bottom. Provided the compost is slightly damp, the compost may be placed in the shade and given no water for ten days. It is possible to strike a number of cuttings in the same pot or box, the best months for doing this being June and July.

Offshoots may be removed in the case of some cacti. This is a necessary operation in the case where the offshoots grow out at various angles to the middle segment of the plant, and improves the parent plant. It isn't necessary to remove offshoots (unless they are needed for propagation) where they spring from the base of the plant.

Cacti may also be propagated by grafting; if the top is cut off an Opuntia, for instance, another cactus may be grafted on if the surface area of the cuts is of a similar size. The two are merely pressed together and tied down, and union will soon take place.

It is also possible to graft by the wedge method.

VARIETIES

There are such a large number of cacti to choose from that it is very difficult to make a small selection. As it is, however, imperative in a book of this character, I have chosen those which grow easily and which are very attractive.

CEREUS

C. azureus – looks like a slender column. Has six ribs and short spines. Young plants have a bluish appearance. *Aporocactus flagelliformis* – commonly known as the Rat's Tail. Has spiny, slender stems and beautiful 3 in. long bright magenta flowers. Should be grown suspended from the roof. *Cepholocereus senilis* – known as the Old Man Cactus. A very popular type. Covered with bristles, and the seedlings are very attractive.

ECHINOCACTUS

E. bicolor – has a large number of spines, and is oval in shape, though it is apt to vary in form and colours. The flowers are to be found even on quite young plants and are large and violet-purple in colour. *Notocactus leninghausii* – this is a very beautiful type, and may become columnar. The plant is covered with bright yellow spines, and there are numbers of ribs. It bears yellow flowers which last quite well. *Rebutia minuscula* – this is a small green plant and has low spiral tubercles. Can be produced from seed, and bears scarlet flowers after two years. *Astrophytum myriostigma* – known as the Bishop's Cap. May have four, five or six ribs, but no spines. It is covered with small white flecks, bears (from the centre) large pale yellow flowers.

ECHINOCEREUS

E. de Laetii – similar to *C. senilis*, and may be known by the name of Old Man too. Is apt to branch from the base. *E. chloranthus* – bears small yellowish flowers, the plant being covered with spines and oval in shape. *E. dasyacanthus* – cylindrical in shape, bearing reddish grey spines, large yellow flowers. *E. stramineus* – grows in groups, and the plants are egg-shaped. Straw-coloured spines and purple flowers.

ECHINOPSIS

E. aurea – small plant bearing yellow flowers and spherical in shape. *E. eyriesii* – bears large white flowers with long tubes. Has been much hybridized.

MAMMILLARIA

M. bombycina – is round or cylindrical, and has a woolly crown. Has small carmine flowers and white fruit, and the spines are white also, though the central ones are reddish. *M. elegans* – also cylindrical. The tubercles are spirally arranged, and bear stars of small spines. Carmine flowers borne in a ring. *M. gracilis* – also known as *M. fragilis*. Has short white spines which are easily broken. Plant itself shaped like a club. *M. plumosa* – small plant with soft spines, giving a feathery effect. Very attractive. *M. schelhasei* – dark green branching type. Inner spines hooked and outer ones soft. Yellow flowers with red stripes. *M. wildii* – small and elongated, dark green. Small flowers, white and quite abundant. Has tiny spines.

OPUNTIA

O. bergeriana – tall plant which has long spines and green leaves. *O. leptocaulis* – has cylindrical stem and long spines. *O. ursina* – commonly known as Grizzly Bear because it has long grey hairs.

PHYLLOCACTUS

P. anguliger – has dark green branches and angled edges, large white, scented flowers. *P. cartagense* – long thin branches, sweetly scented white flowers which open at night. *P. phyllanthus* – leaf-like branches, light green in colour and greenish flowers. *P. stenopetalum* – narrow branches and white flowers. *E. retusa hybrids* – the leaves borne in greyish-green rosettes, beautiful orange and yellow bell-like flowers produced on tall stems.

SEMPERVIVUM

There are large numbers of Sempervivums, many of which are sub-shrubby. In the genus Monanthes the plants are mostly very small with curious greenish-yellow star-like flowers. Those who wish for further lists of cacti and succulents should consult books and catalogues on this subject.

Succulents

All cacti are succulents, but all succulents are not cacti. Amateurs find it easy to recognize the difference between the two of them except perhaps in the case of Euphorbias which have spines and thorns. The succulents store moisture in their foliage or stems and in some cases in their roots. This enables them to overcome long periods of drought. There are hundreds of succulents, and only a short list is given as a guide.

AGAVE

Usually live for a great number of years before producing their flower stalk and then die after throwing up numerous offsets. *A. filifera* – a small plant with greyish-green leaves covered with white stripes, white fibres hang from the leaves. *A. stricta* – bears rosettes of slender round greyish-green foliage. *A. victoriae-reginae* – leaves are dark green, shiny with white stripes.

ALOE

Very similar to the Agave, but the flowering stalk is produced at the side of the rosette. The plant continues to live after flowering. *A. arborescens* – has long toothed foliage. *A. ciliaris* – a semi-climber with small green foliage. *A. distans* – rather tall plant with shortish dark foliage. *A. humilis* – a small growing plant with greyish-green leaves, slightly toothed. *A. variegata* – an attractive plant known as the Partridge Breasted Aloe.

CRASSULA

All members of this group have star-shaped flowers, all of them small. *C. bolusii* – small greyish foliage, covered with brown spots. Bears white flowers. *C. corollina* – has baby foliage, covered with crystal spots. *C. cultrata* – the leaves are tipped with red, the plants are branching, short and dark green. *C. gillii* – leaves are borne in flat dark rosettes. The flowers are white, being borne on long stems. They last for several weeks. *C. multicava* – the round leaves become a bright red if the plant is starved. Pinkish flowers are produced late in winter. *C. pyramidalis* – the leaves are dark green and tightly packed, and seem to form little four-sided columns.

ECHEVERIA

The true Echeveria bear short bell-shaped flowers, the leaves being generally broad. *E. amoena* – the leaves borne in tiny rosettes, being a greyish colour and tinted with red.

EUPHORBIA

All Euphorbias discharge a milky juice when punctured. The flowers are generally insignificant, the stem being column-like. Many have no leaves, and some are thorny. *E. cereiformis* – looks like a cactus, has straight thorns, is tall. *E. gorgonis* – has short branches and depressed crowns. *E. splendens* – very thorny, bears brilliant crimson flowers. Supposed to be the plant from which Our Lord's cross of thorns was made.

MESEMBRYANTHEMUM

Perhaps the best flowering group of succulents, and the largest. Very varied. There are so many types to choose from, that I have not attempted to do so. Special note should, however, be made of the genus Conophytum where most of the plants look like little brown or green pebbles, and which rest in the summer and look dead. The genus Didymaetus looks like an inverted boat with a V-slice cut in the centre. The genus Lithops also looks like stones which have flat cleft tops. The genus Rimaria has pairs of leaves pressed together forming a semi-globose whitish green body.

16 Month by month in the greenhouse

JANUARY
General Prepare composts and receptacles ready for sowing seeds and taking cuttings. Top-dress stove plants which do not need repotting. Begin to force bulbs for flowering in March; also early-flowering shrubs such as Daphnes and Azaleas. Start standard Fuchsias in heat and bring in first batch of pot Roses for forcing. Sponge leaves of foliage plants. Remove decaying leaves and dead flowers. Hot water pipes may be painted and glass cleaned if necessary. *Potting* Pot on seedlings and rooted cuttings as they need it. Repot and start into growth Achimenes, Begonias, Gloxinias and Hippeastrums. Repot or top-dress Cypripediums. *Propagation* (a) Seeds: during the second half of the month sow seeds of Abutilon, Acacia, Annuals, Asparagus Fern, Balsams, Begonias, Cannas, Clerodendron, Coleus, Eucalyptus, Freesia, Fuchsia, Gloxinia, Grevillea, Leucocoryne, Pelargonium, Petunia, Saintpaulia, Solanum and Streptocarpus. (b) Vegetative: take cuttings of Carnations, Chrysanthemums, Coleus, Fuchsia, Heliotrope, Impatiens, Jacobinia, Lantana, Pelargonium, Salvia and Tradescantia. *Pruning* Prune pot Roses, Fuchsias, Bougainvillea, Passion Flowers, Plumbago and many of the climbers. *Temperature* In the ordinary greenhouse maintain a night temperature of 40–45°F and a day one of 50–55°F. *Watering* Water sparingly, being careful not to wet the flowers of plants in bloom.

FEBRUARY
General Introduce more bulbs and Roses into heat for forcing. Bring into warmer house Heliotrope and Hydrangeas. Start Gloriosas into growth. Prick out seedlings when large enough. Continue cleaning glass. *Potting* Repot or top-dress plants starting into growth, such as Fuchsias, Pelargoniums, Ferns and foliage plants. Pot on young plants as they need it. Pot up rooted cuttings, Lily bulbs, Gloxinias and Begonias. Repot Odontoglossums as they finish flowering. Repot Thunias and start into growth. *Propagation* (a) Seeds: sow seeds of Alonsoa,

179

Annuals, Calceolarias, Carnations, Celosias, Celsias, Hippeastrums, Oxalis, Primulas, Salvias, Tecomas and Thunbergias. (b) Vegetative: take cuttings of Acalyphas, Begonias, Bouvardias, Marguerites, Petunias, Pileas and Saintpaulias. Take leaf cuttings of Begonia Gloire de Lorraine. *Temperature* As for January. *Ventilation* Give some ventilation during the middle of bright, mild sunny days. *Watering* Water more freely as the days begin to lengthen.

MARCH

General Bring in more bulbs for forcing. Divide Cannas and start into growth. Start Caladiums and Crinums into growth in heat. Prick out seedlings as they become large enough. Stake tall growing plants, fumigate or spray pot Roses if aphis is present. Shade plants from sudden bursts of bright sunshine. *Potting* Continue to pot on plants as they require it and pot up seedlings and rooted cuttings. Repot Orchids, e.g. Calanthes, as they begin to grow. Repot Cacti and Succulents if they need it. Pot up more Lilies. *Propagation* (a) Seeds: sow seeds of Annuals, Aralia, Cacti, Cascade Chrysanthemums, Rehmannia and several shrubs. (b) Vegetative: take cuttings of Abutilon, Coronilla, Cytisus, Echeveria, Euphorbia, Habrothamnus, Hydrangea, Panicum, Plumbago, Ruellia, Selaginella, Sparmannia, Streptosolen, Trachelium and other softwooded plants. Take leaf cuttings of Echeveria. *Pruning* Prune Bouvardias as they finish flowering. *Temperature* In the ordinary greenhouse maintain a night temperature of 45–50°F and a day one of 55–60°F. *Ventilation* Ventilate as soon as the temperature reaches 65°F. *Watering* Syringe plants, except those in flower, morning and evening.

APRIL

General Bulbs which have flowered may be placed in a cold frame to harden off. Stand Roses outside after flowering. Prick out seedlings as they become large enough. Fumigate to destroy insect pests. Shade during the day. *Potting* Pot on or pot up plants as they need it. Repot Indian Azaleas and Camellias directly after flowering. Repot or top-dress Abutilons, Aloysias, Epacrises and ivy-leaved Pelargoniums. *Propagation* (a) Seeds: sow seeds of Cinerarias and any others mentioned for March. (b) Vegetative: take cuttings of Achimenes, Epacris, Eranthemum, Euphorbia, Mimulus, Poinsettias and other soft-wooded plants. *Temperature* As for

March. *Ventilation* Open the ventilators early in the morning and shut down early in the afternoon. *Watering* Syringe plants, except those in flower. Start to water Cacti freely. Gradually withhold water from Freesias and Hippeastrums as they finish flowering.

MAY

General Carnations, Cyclamen, Primulas and Arums may be stood outside in cold frames. Stand Chrysanthemums outside. Top-dress Lilies as they require it. Prick out seedlings. Stake and tie in plants as they need it. Shade plants from strong sunlight. Fumigate frequently to keep down insect pests. Any repainting can be started as soon as is convenient. *Potting* Summer flowering plants should be put into their final pots, also Chrysanthemums, by the middle of the month. Pot up rooted cuttings, and seedlings, and pot on plants that require it. Repot Cassias, Ericas and Acacias. *Propagation* (a) Seeds: sow seeds of Balsams, Calceolarias, Grevillea, *Humea elegans*, Oxalis and Primulas. (b) Vegetative: take cuttings of Azaleas, Centradenia, Coleus thyrsoides, Ericas, Pycnostachys and other soft-wooded plants. *Pruning* Cut back Acacias. Cut back Poinsettias, and start to grow in heat. *Temperature* As for April. *Ventilation* Ventilate freely, leaving a little air on at night in very mild weather. *Watering* Water freely. The floors should be damped down twice a day, and the staging and pots syringed to maintain a moist atmosphere.

JUNE

General Gradually harden off forced shrubs and plant outside. Prick out seedlings when they are large enough. Dry off Tritonias, Nerines and Freesias. Fumigate or spray to get rid of aphides. Shade from sun. Make out seed list for plants to sow in the autumn. *Potting* Pot plants as they require it. Finish potting on Chrysanthemums into finals. *Propagation* (a) Seeds: sow Gloxinias, Begonias and Thunbergias, and any mentioned for May. (b) Vegetative: take cuttings of Acacias, Coronilla, Datura, Hydrangea, Thunbergia, Veronica, Crassula and other succulents. Layer Hoya and Malmaison Carnations. Side graft Camellias. *Pruning* Cut back Hydrangeas lightly to remove old flowering heads. *Temperature* Artificial heat will only be required in stove house. Cooler houses may need a little in cold or damp weather. *Ventilation* Allow plenty of air. *Watering* Water freely, twice a day if necessary in hot weather.

Damp paths frequently and syringe foliage plants. Cannas need plenty of water.

JULY
General Stand pot Azaleas, Ericas, Camellias, Acacias, Hydrangeas and Rhododendrons outside in a sheltered spot. Stake and tie in Chrysanthemums and top-dress. Prick out seedlings. Top-dress Lilies again. Shade from sun. Fumigate and spray when necessary. Order bulbs for forcing. This is a good time to paint the inside of the houses as the plants may be stood outside. *Potting* Repot and start Freesias. Repot Cytisus and Coronilla and plunge outside. Pot plants as they need it. Perpetual Carnations should go into their final pots. *Propagation* (a) Seeds: sow Mignonette and Nicotiana for winter flowering. Sow Salpiglossis and Stocks for spring flowering. Sow Freesias and Nierembergias. (b) Vegetative: take cuttings of Abutilons, Calceolarias, Ixoras and any mentioned last month. Bud Orange and Lemon trees. *Pruning* Cut back Coronilla, Cytisus, Nierembergias and show Pelargoniums. *Temperature* As for June. *Ventilation* Give plenty of air, leaving a little on at night. *Watering* Water freely and keep the atmosphere moist, especially where ferns and foliage plants are grown.

AUGUST
General Prick out seedlings. Finish top dressing Chrysanthemums, and tie in and disbud. Remove buds from winter flowering Pelargoniums. Keep houses well shaded. *Potting* Repot Arums and Cyclamen. Pot plants as they require it, Primulas should be ready for their final pots. Start to pot up early flowering bulbs, such as Roman Hyacinths, etc. *Propagation* (a) Seeds: sow seeds of Annuals for spring flowering and Cyclamen. (b) Vegetative: take cuttings of Aloysia, Begonias, Eupatorium, Fuchsias, Heliotrope, Panicum, Petunias, Pelargoniums, Pilea, Salvias, Selaginella, Trachelium and any other soft-wooded plants which are available. *Temperature* As for July. *Ventilation* As for July. *Watering* As for July. Syringe plants standing outside each evening during hot weather.

SEPTEMBER
General Bring inside and top-dress Azaleas, Ericas, Camellias, etc. Bring in Chrysanthemums, winter-flowering Pelargoniums and Salvias. Continue to tie in and disbud Chrysanthe-

mums. Prick out seedlings. Stake those plants which need it. Less shading will be required and temporary shading may be washed off at the end of the month. *Potting* Pot up bulbs including some Lilies. Pot up Malmaison Carnation layers and take inside. Pot plants which require it, Cinerarias should go into their final pots. *Propagation* (a) Seeds: sow more Annuals. (b) Vegetative: take cuttings of Crotons, Fittonia, Saintpaulia and Tradescantia. *Pruning* Prune hard-wooded climbers as they finish flowering, e.g. Streptosolen, Plumbago, etc. *Temperature* Maintain a night temperature of 45°F in the ordinary greenhouse. Some artificial heat will be required at night. *Ventilation* Ventilate freely during the middle of the day, but give none at night, except during mild weather. *Watering* Water less and keep atmosphere drier. Syringe and sponge all foliage plants.

OCTOBER

General Bring into house Cinerarias, Cyclamen and Primulas. Store Caladiums and Gloxinias on their sides under the staging when they have dried off. Store tuberous Begonias, Cannas and Lilies in a frost-proof shed. Disbud Carnations. Top dress annuals and pinch back to encourage bushy growth. Prick off seedlings. Stake plants where necessary. Fumigate and wash glass on the inside. Remove all shading. Overhaul the heating apparatus. *Potting* Repot Roses and stand outside. Finish potting up bulbs. Pot up Dielytra and stand in a cold frame. Pot plants which need it. *Propagation* (a) Seeds: sow seeds of Celsia for summer flowering. (b) Vegetative: take cuttings of foliage plants. *Pruning* Prune Oleanders and pot Roses. Continue to prune climbers. *Temperature* Maintain in the greenhouse a night temperature of 40–45°F and a day one of 55°F. *Ventilation* Give a little air in the late morning and early afternoon on sunny days. *Watering* Water sparingly. Gradually withhold water from tuberous Begonias, Gloxinias, Lilies and Oleanders. No syringing is necessary in the greenhouse.

NOVEMBER

General Top-dress Clivias and move into a warm house. Prick out seedlings. Start to force earliest bulbs. Bring in Hydrangeas. Stake plants which need it. Scrub woodwork and paint pipes if necessary. Clean the glass on the outside of the houses. Wash all empty pots, etc. *Potting* Repot Lilies and put in cold frame until growth starts. Repot if necessary and start Hippeastrums.

Pot plants which require it. *Propagation* Vegetative: start to take cuttings of Carnations and Chrysanthemums. *Pruning* Finish pruning Datura, Oleander, Plumbago and other climbers. *Temperature* In the greenhouse maintain a night temperature of 40–45°F and a day one of 50–55°F. *Ventilation* Admit air only when the sun is shining. *Watering* Water sparingly. Cacti and Succulents should be kept dry. Very little syringing is necessary in the stove house.

DECEMBER

General Bring in more bulbs for forcing. Start to force Hydrangeas and early-flowering shrubs. Cut down Chrysanthemums which have flowered and stand pots in frames. Thin and top-dress annuals in pots and stake where necessary. Fumigate where aphides are present. Remove dead leaves and flowers. Paint staging if necessary. *Potting* Pot up Lily bulbs. Pot plants where necessary. *Propagation* Vegetative: continue to take Carnation and Chrysanthemum cuttings. *Temperature* As for November. *Ventilation* Give a little air whenever possible. *Watering* Water cautiously. Syringe very little in the stove house.

17 Pests and diseases

Naturally before discussing the control of individual pests and diseases some mention must be made first of all of what may be called Greenhouse Hygiene. Every year hundreds of plants are lost merely because of uncleanliness in the greenhouse. It is important, therefore, to see that the inside of the house is washed down at least once a year with cresylic acid, using 1 pint of this chemical to 12 gallons of water and stirring in $1\frac{1}{2}$ oz of a liquid spreader which you can use instead of soft soap if you prefer. If you can take the plants out of the house for a day or two you could give the inside a really good spraying.

Then much can be done with the more permanent crops like vines and peaches by fumigation in the winter. Fumigation is also useful in the spring and summer to control certain pests like the white fly on tomatoes, and the simplest way of doing this is to use a proprietary cyanide powder such as Cyanogas or Cyandie. These should be used in accordance with instructions given on the tins but it means sprinkling $\frac{1}{4}$ oz of the powder along the floor of the house for every 1,000 ft of cubic capacity.

It is most important to have a damp floor, but the leaves of the plants concerned dry, when fumigating in summer and it is equally important to open the house up very early, in the morning before the sunshine gets on to the plants. However, when you buy the special cyanide powder you will, as I have already said, be careful to follow the instructions on the packet.

SPREADERS
We use soft soap to cause a wash to spread more evenly and to help a nicotine wash to be more effective.

THE CONTROL OF WHITEFLIES AND RED SPIDERS BY PREDATORS
The Whitefly Parasite (Encarsia formosa). This is a small wasp with a black thorax and yellow abdomen. The adults can fly actively. The parasite will lay its eggs in fairly mature whitefly

185

scales. The eggs hatch within the whitefly scales in four days and the larvae feed for a further eight days before pupating and turning the whitefly scale black. The adult parasite will emerge ten days later. The rate of development is affected by temperature, being longer at lower and shorter at higher temperatures. The parasite does not feed on plant material or on other sects. Its survival is entirely dependent on the presence of whitefly. The parasite is best used as soon as the first whiteflies appear.

The Red Spider Predator (Phytoseiulus persimilis). The predator is fast moving and orange in colour. Each female lays approximately 50–60 eggs at 3–4 per day. They hatch in 2–3 days and there are 3 immature stages. The complete life-cycle takes 7 days, about half the time of the red spider mite. It is very efficient at searching for its prey and each female will devour up to 5 adults or 30 eggs and young per day. It does not feed on plant material, and its survival is entirely dependent on the maintenance of the red spider mite population. Unlike its host, the predator does not normally hibernate during the winter months, and must be reintroduced each year as required.

Introduction rate. The following estimates are based on the small amateur glasshouse of a size, say, 6 ft × 8 ft.

The Whitefly Parasite: If the whitefly population is low use 1,000 parasites. If the whitefly population is high use 1,000 parasites, followed by a second introduction of another 1,000 a fortnight later.

The Red Spider Predator: Use 100 predators per house, unless the infestation is very high, when 200 should be used.

WHERE TO BUY

These predators may be obtained from The Organic Growers Ltd., Longridge, Creeting Road, Stowmarket, Suffolk IP14 5BT.

Full details of all garden pests and diseases, and how to deal with them, are given in the appropriate volume of my Basic Books series.

Index